My Search For Dogman: Nature's Scariest Cryptid (A Scholarly Analysis)

Jim Hoffmann

Susquehanna Road Publishing

Apple Valley, California

The High Desert of SoCal

© 2021 by Jim Hoffmann. All rights reserved. No portion of this book may be reproduced, stored in a retrieval system, or transmitted in any form or by any means – electronic, mechanical, photocopy, recording, or any other type – except for brief quotations in printed reviews, without the permission of the author or Susquehanna Road Publishing.

Furthermore, the publisher is pretty sure that the information depicted in this story is true. HOWEVER, it could be argued that any similarity to any person living or dead, including the author, is merely coincidental. But, hey - mistakes do happen.

KDP ISBN: 9798710397015

Unless otherwise noted, the author and the publisher make no explicit guarantees as to the accuracy of the information contained in this book, and in some cases the names of people and places have been altered to protect their privacy.

Cover Photo Credit: "Dogman Redux" © 2021 Johnny R. Vaile. All rights reserved. Used with permission.

Lupus Aeternam Composite: Original imagery © 2021 Erin Johnson and Johnny Vaile respectively. All rights reserved. Used with permission. Composite created by and © 2021 Jim Hoffmann. All rights reserved.

Printed in the United States of America. This book is printed on good, old American paper with good, old American ingenuity.

I edited this entire book. Any mistakes are wholly mine, and I duly apologize. Although

I strive for perfection, unless you're God or a typical politician, it's just a concept.

OTHER WORKS BY JIM HOFFMANN...

My Search for 'Shock Me': Ace Frehley's Signature Song (A Scholarly Analysis) [2020]; *My Search for 'Niki Hoeky': Granddaddy of Swamp Rock (A Scholarly Analysis)* [2020]; *King Kong Pete: Redbone and Beyond* with Pete De Poe (2017); *Come And Get Your Love* with Pat "Redbone" Vegas (2017); *Lattie McGee and Dr. Gottfried* with Charles J. Stecker, Jr. and O.R. Rutledge (2016); *International Pop Overthrow: The Golden Triangle of Power Pop - Material Issue* (2015); *Adolph Kuhn: An American Journey* with Adolph Kuhn (2010); *The Boy in the Box: America's Unknown Child* (1st ed. 2007, 2nd ed. 2012, 3rd ed. 2018).

DEDICATION

To my precious wife and kids. The one thing I've done right. You always deserved way more than I could provide....

ACKNOWLEDGEMENTS

To my inspiring teachers: Mrs. Odle, Mrs. Kutashi, and Mrs. Schroeder, Dr. Schlauch, Dr. Miess, and Dr. Horak.

To my mentors, Paul Bakas ("Sensei" to my "Grasshopper"), and Jim Fowler.

To Pat "Redbone" Vegas, Pete De Poe, and my agent, CJ Silberman of the Fairy Forest Agency, for giving me a chance.

To my colleague and friend, Heather Alexander - the best administrative secretary I've ever worked with - for reading the manuscript critically, and making cogent suggestions to make it the best possible.

To my historical "partner in crime" and friend, Mark Guererro - the "Scribe of Chicano Rock" (MarkGuerrero.com) - for reading the manuscript critically, and making cogent suggestions to make it the best possible.

To artists Erin Johnson and Johnny R. Vaile for their emotive contributions to this work.

To "Mr. Black" for your bravery and persistence in working to better understand these strange creatures so that we all might be better off.

To all of the brave podcasters who risked their reputations, social stations, and livelihoods to share the nectar of knowledge on the Dogman, Werewolf, and Bigfoot.

To my now eternally distant Dad - whom I hardly knew. Life is not about what others say about you, but what you say about yourself. For who you are matters - what others say about you does not. Those who love you know, those who don't, don't.

You were an imperfectly devoted son, brother, father, grandfather, newspaperman, a damn good truck driver, writer, satirist, community volunteer, mentor, and devoted Follower of Christ. So, I say with pain in my heart, but pride in my soul . . . You will be sorely missed. (James Vernon Hoffmann, Sr., Wednesday, May 13, 1942 to Friday, March 9, 2019 . . . RIP....

And most importantly, Jesus Christ,
my Lord and Savior....

EPIGRAPH

Eric Clapton, Singer/Songwriter, Rock God

"I'm an egomaniac with an inferiority complex."[1]

Bob Dylan, Singer/Songwriter, Rock God

The artist should be "constantly in a state of becoming. As long as you stay in that realm, you'll sort of be alright."[2]

Abraham Lincoln, Lawyer, Politician, Great Thinker

---

[1] TrueBlueCdnEh, "Classic 60 Minutes - Eric Clapton," YouTube, May 10, 2020 (2:58-3:01). Retrieved 11/21/2020: https://www.youtube.com/watch?v=ekT2Df1iZCE.

[2] Dylan, Bob, *No Direction Home*, Paramount Pictures (Distributor), Directed by Martin Scorcese, 2005.

"Always bear in mind that your own resolution to succeed is more important than any other one thing."[3]

Glee Character Rachel Berry (Lea Michelle)

"He [Mr. Schuester, aka "Mr. Schue"] taught me the one great thing that all teachers do - and there are *so* many of them out there - and that is being a part of something special does not make you special. Something is special because *you* are a part of it."[4]

Danny Thomas, Entertainer

Danny Thomas, one of the greatest humanitarians ever, took life by the horns,

---

[3] Brainy Quote, "Abraham Lincoln Quotes," BrainyQuote.com. Retrieved 12/13/2020: https://www.brainyquote.com/quotes/abraham_lincoln_10927 4.

[4] Wikipedia: Dreams Come True (Glee). The very last episode of *Glee*, "Dreams Come True," March 20, 2015, Season 6, Episode 13. Of course, Mr. Schuester was played by Matthew Morrison. Beware: This is a tear jerker! Being a teacher by trade, it's exceptionally so.

yet stayed humble and grateful to God. He famously prayed for the Lord's intervention in his life . . . "Show me my way in life and I will build you a shrine."[5] In fact, to show his appreciation for God's work *in his life*, he founded the children's hospital, St. Jude's. Interestingly, St. Jude Thaddeus is the patron saint of lost causes.

---

[5] See StJude.org about Danny Thomas' most important contribution to the world. He definitely "made a dent in the universe," as Steve Jobs would say. If you can find it in your heart, please donate to this organization. What a powerful testament to loving our World's hurting children whom you don't even know. Yet, God Knows....

FOREWORD

I first became aware of Dogman through my father, Jim Hoffmann, and his conversations with me about *Dogman Encounters Radio*. (For Christmas of 2019, I even bought him a shirt from the podcast merch site.) Interestingly, I never listened directly to any podcasts, rather I gathered my information about Dogman from what my father told me.

I distinctly remember him talking about the Upper New York State case where a man was driving a quad-type vehicle and the Dogman was running alongside it. [*Dogman Encounters Radio* Episode 190 out of Cato, New York.]

Admittedly, my father and I differ on what a Dogman really is. I think it's a paranormal creature that manifests. In other words, I do not believe it's a living, breathing creature. I think it's paranormal such as a demon - straight from Hell. It is somehow able to manifest using our energy.

Again, Dogman is not a real creature - like a Bigfoot.

Though I don't necessarily fear the Dogman's existence, I do think my father is spreading awareness of this creature, and is helping people to open their minds to Dogman - and other cryptids - which inhabit our planet. This is good for if someone encounters the Dogman, and it's a threat, that person can be better prepared for it.

Devinne Jean Hoffmann[6]
Apple Valley, California
Sunday, January 31, 2021

---

[6] My beautiful and smart daughters are way more talented than I could ever be. They get that from their mother, truthfully. I'm so proud of them. Devinne's works, "Tween Dramas." which are appropriate for 4th-6th grade (*The Odd Couple, The Time to Remember,* and *The Story of Us*), can be purchased on Amazon.

PROLOGUE

It's just you and me here, and I want to tell you a story. I honestly do not expect you to believe me, and wholeheartedly respect you if you don't. I still have my doubts. Please . . . when you are ready, take my hand and let me guide you to the fire of your desire to be frightened. Be careful to step over the bones of your previous fears. Don't disturb them! It's going to be scary enough. Now, sit down next to me and this seering, rhetorical, roaring fire of fear in the deep, dark forest of our minds.

Oh, I forgot to suggest that before you commit - grab a drink and a smoke and a snack, preferably one that does not stain the pages of this book, and then let me tell you a crazy and zany and sometimes frightening series of stories - which will eventually lead our restless souls and indubitable fears down a narrow pathway. Try not to get too close to the treeline. Try not to be the last one in line. Hurry! Stay close to one another. Dogman, after all, is elusive and always, always - no matter the distance separating us - within our grasp.

Yes, this tale is "My Search For Dogman," but I'm taking *you* with me. Together, we will seek out and discover this wholly strange cryptid, an apex predator known as Dogman, but neither you nor I can close our eyes. It's all in and all open. So, try not to be too afraid, and enjoy this true horror story. A final word of caution. This accounting is not all inclusive, rather it's just a primer for the average Dogman enthusiast, curious seeker of primal fear, or any and all discerning readers.

INTRODUCTION

Lon Chaney, Jr. is no Dogman - but he did scare the Hell out of me.

When I was a kid growing up in the suburbs of Chicago, Illinois, in a little bedroom suburb called Glendale Heights, radio and television were a big part of our lives. We were lucky, too, that there was a lot of quality programming on the airwaves "back in the day." I used to listen to WLS Radio with disc jockey Larry Lujack[7], one of the greatest of all time, and the original "shock jock," along with Steve Dahl, at the Loop (WLUP).[8]

But, more to the point of this treatise, on Saturday nights, my brother, sister, and I would gather on the rough patterned green couch in our basement at the 1500 block of Ardmore Avenue, down the street from our quaint little Charles G. Reskin Elementary School, and watch one of the most feared

---

[7] Wikipedia: Larry Lujack.
[8] Wikipedia: Steve Dahl.

television programs of all time, at least according to any kid, *Creature Features*.[9]

Literally turning our TV dial to Channel 9 (WGN) with real fingers, and a real twist of the wrist, and not some remote control, let alone a smartphone, we commenced one of the world's greatest rituals: watching - enduring - a scary movie. I recall this show was on Saturday nights around 10 PM.

We also watched the heralded *Svengoolie* on Channel 32 (WFLD)[10], but this tended to take a ludicrous look at horror films (with its comedic host, Svengoolie), and so by doing, it softened the "scare factor" of the film that night. As I recall, some of the films tended to be more of the "B Film" types, and less scary, like *Abbott and Costello Meet Frankenstein*. I recall that *Svengoolie* aired on Friday nights around 10 PM.

---

[9] Wikipedia: Creature Features.
[10] Wikipedia: Svengoolie.

Oh, the horror films which we were able to enjoy! My favorite ones were the classics, though: *Frankenstein* (Boris Karloff), *Dracula* (Bela Lagosi), *The Mummy* (Boris Karloff), and of course, *The Wolfman* (Lon Chaney, Jr.).[11]

So, my perspective of the Wolfman, or werewolf, was carved into my brain and my soul forever by the haunting portrayal of Chaney. One of this film's most famous scenes, and one of the scariest and creepiest of all time, was watching the Wolfman creep through the fog-laden countryside (LOL . . . In reality a soundstage at Universal Studios), enroute to another victim.

Another, Chaney's magnanimous transformation from man to beast before the awestruck audience. The art of filmmaking does not get any better than that, even with today's advanced technological and cinematic tricks. I must admit, though, that the process in the film,

---

[11] Wikipedia: Frankenstein (1931 Film), Dracula (1931 English Language Film), The Mummy (1932 Film), and The Wolfman (1941 Film).

An American Werewolf in London, ranks right up there.[12] *The Wolfman's* Intro is predicated upon "huge scary." A ticker tile scrolls along a trembling message:

> "The Legend of the Damned
> in many a distant
> village there exists
> the legend of the
> werewolf or Wolf
> man...a legend of
> a strange mortal
> man with the hair
> and fangs of an
> unearthly beast....
> his hideous howl
> a dirge of death-"[13]

---

[12] Fear: The Home of Horror. "Iconic Wolfman Transformation Scene | An American Werewolf in London," March 28, 2020. Retrieved 11/7/2020: https://www.youtube.com/watch?v=GHyvfOUEK4o.

[13] YouTube Movies, "The Wolf Man (1941)," April 20, 2011. Retrieved 11/7/2020: https://www.youtube.com/watch?v=bhVgSUI-moM.

I mean, "dirge of death!" Do you remember those days of watching scary movies? Hmm. And then, along came *Dogman Encounters Radio*....

CH I: ORIGINS OF MY DOGMAN PASSION

I want to be clear again: this is *not* exhaustive research to lay at your feet all that's known about the Dogman creature. It *is* a primer of the subject intended to introduce said topic to those discerning readers - *you* - who have this primal taste for the creatures but know very little thereof. So...

"What the hell is a Dogman? That cannot be real!" This was my reaction when I first heard Vic Cundiff's *Dogman Encounters Radio* (hereafter DER)[14] podcast back in October of 2018. Believe me, I actually laughed for several weeks when the topic of Dogman crossed my mind. It was that unbelievable to me. So . . . What is a Dogman? Is it real?

---

[14] *Dogman Encounters Radio*, a weekly podcast on Fridays (YouTube), was established by Vic Cundiff on June 23, 2014. I cannot imagine what got him into this business, but, what an interesting topic.

There is no clear definition of a Dogman. Wikipedia does not even directly reference it, although there are pages for Werewolf, Beast of Bray Road, and Michigan Dogman. My best definition is that a Dogman is essentially a creature, flesh and blood and/or spiritual - depending on the interpretation, which looks like a wolf or dog, can walk on two legs like a man, is scary, and can be dangerous as Hell. Think: Lon Chaney, Jr. in *The Wolf Man* (1941) or Hugh Jackman in *Van Helsing* (2004). Either way, monsters are apparently real.

I wish I could remember the exact episode, but I believe it was one of DER's less well-known, although equally interesting, episodes. In fact, while listening recently to Episode 21, I believe this could be the first Dogman account of any kind which I have ever heard.[15]

---

[15] Dogman Encounters Radio, "I Shot a Dogman with a .30-06 Rifle! (Dogman Encounters Episode 21)," YouTube, February 17, 2015. Retrieved 11/9/2020: https://www.youtube.com/watch?v=YIVn-GJJxYk.

Like an apex predator, *Dogman Encounters Radio* crept into the cryptic scene in 2014, currently has roughly 70K subscribers, and almost 23 million views as of this writing. But, does Dogman really exist? These eyewitnesses are either liars, crazy, or there is some truth to their stories. They cannot all be lying or misinterpreting what they're seeing.

I was - and still am - stunned and, as is per normal with my undiagnosed ADHD, obsessed with this topic. I thought about Dogman constantly, every waking moment, as the adage goes, and discussed it with people when these gracious souls would listen to my banter about this creature. Indubitably, my family and colleagues could probably verify this, even pinpoint the moment this obsession started. Nope. I couldn't get the Dogman concept - and whether or not it's real - out of my mind. Plain and simple. Still can't.

Now, a point of distinction: the Dogman is considered an animal, as opposed to a Werewolf which, by tradition, is a person who turns into this creature "during a full moon" or at night, although there are accounts of Werewolves transforming from human to creature during the day.[16]

Another point of distinction, it's interesting to peruse the Internet on the topic of "cryptids." I never imagined the vast and varying types "known to man."[17] Bear in mind that this type of cryptid creature, the Dogman, in modern American Culture, undoubtedly has varying forms and labels throughout the world.

For example, a popularly known creature, which is similar to the Dogman in

---

[16] Ask Any Difference, "Difference Between Lycan and Werewolf (With Table)," AskAnyDifferecne.com, Date Unknown. Retrieved 11/25/2020: https://askanydifference.com/difference-between-lycan-and-werewolf/. My intention with this work is not to get too technical. Lycan? Werewolf? The distinctions are beyond me, although this source states they are very similar in nature. The point is, Lycans can transform anytime, whereas Werewolves cannot.
[17] Wikipedia: List of Cryptids.

looks, are the Wendigo[18] (evil spiritual being) and Skinwalker[19] (a witch who turns into an animal like a large dog) - both which terrorize Native American people just as effectively. Lest we forget, Cajun Culture down in the swamps of Louisiana has the Rougarou[20], a traditional werewolf - a human who changes into an animal.

The Native American connection to Dogman seems clear. Check out author Linda Godfrey's groundbreaking book, *The Beast of Bray Road* (2014). I affectionately dub Godfrey, the "Dogmother of the Dogman Tale."[21] She discovered in her

---

[18] Dogman Narratives, "Strange Wendigo Skinwalker Sighting (Wendigo Narratives)," YouTube, December 27, 2017. Retrieved 11/11/2020: https://www.youtube.com/watch?v=Dmt6k0cm7Jg. See also Wikipedia: Wendigo.

[19] Dogman Narratives, "Navajo Skinwalker Native American Stories - Dogman Narratives," YouTube, July 26, 2019. Retrieved 11/11/2020: https://www.youtube.com/watch?v=H_tvwRkCRaU. See also Wikipedia: Skin-Walker.

[20] Wikipedia: Rougarou.

[21] Wisconsin DPI - Resources for the Field, "Linda Godfrey's Writing Process (Wisconsin Writes)," YouTube, April 5, 2016. Retrieved 11/11/2020: https://www.youtube.com/watch?v=fopg9gZ5M_0. Godfrey discusses her writing process, which I find interesting. Are you

research basic variables to most Dogman sightings, what I've dubbed the "Linda Godfrey Variables": Water, Woods, Corn, and Native American Accoutrements.

She argues that most Dogman sightings take place near one or more of these "common threads": water, woods, corn fields, and Native American historical locations. Here it is...

DOGMAN SIGHTING SCALE OF RELIABILITY

Dogman Sighting Scale of Reliability © 2019 Jim Hoffmann. All rights reserved.

Valid. Level Of Character-istics	SIGHT	ING	CHA	RAC	TER	IST	ICS
OPTIMUM (4)	ABNOR	MAL	RANGE	NOR	MAL	RA	NGE
HIGH (3)							

---

considering becoming a writer? Check out her tips. Check out LindaGodfrey.com for more information on this amazing researcher and writer.

	NORM	AL	RANGE	AB	NOR	MAL	RANG E
MED (2)	NORM	AL	RANGE	AB	NOR	MAL	RANG E
LOW (1)							
	(A) Light- ing	(B) Prox- imity	(C) State of Mind	(D) Quali ty of De- tails	(E) Quan tity of De- tails	(F) P.F. Wit- ness Relia bility	(G) Acuity of Loca- tion LGVs

Explanation of Validity Level of Characteristics

All things being equal, it is assumed that each sighting will have a series of characteristics related in the above categories and that they will have a certain value, or validity level, Low, Medium, High, and Optimum. Each is assigned a point value which is purely arbitrary. It is assumed that an average score of 2.0 and above would be the minimal score needed to be considered valid.

Two Color Scheme

Green = normal range
Red = abnormal

Characteristics A-C would be expected to be low scores (Low to Medium, or 1-2 points). Lighting, Proximity to the Dogman, and the witness's State of Mind would all be considered tenuous at best on average. In other words, one would not normally have excellent lighting during an encounter, closeness to the dogman, and a placid state of mind. On the contrary, if a witness scored extremely high within these characteristics, the sighting would have a strong indication of being invalid - if not fake or made up, whether intentional or not.

Characteristics D-G would be expected to be high scores (High to Optimum, 3-4 points). Quality and Quantity of Details, Prima Facie Witness Reliability, and the Acuity of the Location viz-a-viz the four Linda Godfrey Variables: Native American Accoutrements, Corn, Woods, and Water -

all would be considered strong at the least on average. On the contrary, if a witness scored extremely low within these characteristics, the sighting would have a strong indication of being invalid - if not fake or made up, whether intentional or not.

Sighting Characteristics

Lighting (A)
Proximity to Dogman (B)
State of Mind of Witness (C)
Quality of Details (D)
Quantity of Details (E)
Prima Facie Witness Reliability (F)
Acuity of Location (G): Linda Godfrey
Variables: Water, Woods, Corn, and Native American Accoutrements

The topic of a dogman on the surface may sound silly, but there are many people the world over who claim to have encountered these creatures. The Michigan Dogman[22] is one, and even includes a purported fraudulent home movie and a nicely produced jingle, "The Legend."[23] The

---

[22] Wikipedia: Michigan Dogman.

[23] Snookscp, "The Legend of Dogman Song," YouTube, July 1, 2008. Retrieved 11/9/2020: https://www.youtube.com/watch?v=5uwFZYCwnS0. Disc Jockey Steve Cook, a wacky entertainer, released this on April Fool's Day in 1987. Though the song was designed to poke fun at the Dogman legend, if anything, it spurred it on and helped proliferate it.

Beast of Bray Road (in Southern Wisconsin) is another.[24]

I grew up in Glendale Heights, Illinois, in the late 1960s-1970s. On many weekends, my maternal grandparents would drive us up to "the summer home" in Silver Lake, Wisconsin, some 60 miles north along the border of Illinois and Wisconsin. In reality, it was my maternal great-grandparents' home. By the 1970s, that home had been sold and my maternal grandfather, after my maternal grandmother passed away in August of 1982, bought another "summer home" in tiny Salem, Wisconsin, just west of Paddock Lake where my mom and sister live today.

Bray Road, in Elkhorn, Wisconsin, is located only some 25 miles northwest of Salem/Paddock Lake. Perhaps an interesting side note is that my late father told me we would hang out at a house in Lake Geneva in the late 1960s and early 1970s, and that Papa Bear George Halas, the

---

[24] Wikipedia: Beast of Bray Road.

former coach and owner of the Chicago Bears was there, too. I do know that my maternal Great Uncle Charles Nehmzow (my Grandma's brother) married Alice Halas, the niece of Papa Bear. Perhaps that is why.

Let's get back to the task at hand: What is a Dogman and is it real? This depends on who you want to believe, I suppose. There are so many sources out there today, and each has its own unique spin.

The Dogman creature is frightening on so many levels. Their prevalence in society is more widespread than you would expect. Did you know: There are accounts of a Dogman killing a human? Dogman sightings have occurred in urban areas? There have been several credible images[25] taken of the Dogman, too?

I stumbled across a fascinating interview involving famed UFO researchers

[25] Bedtime Stories, "The Michigan Dogman," YouTube, February 23, 2020 (4:08-7:18). Retrieved 11/25/2020: https://www.youtube.com/watch?v=hHqfLhZicdw.

and writers Linda Moulton Howe and Richard Dolan.[26] This eyewitness, Anonymous, claims to have been part of an intelligence group which was privy to UFO research and technology.

His recounting of how President Eisenhower threatened the Area 51 command with invasion of the base by the 1st Army *if they refused to share their intelligence with the President.* Let that sink in for a moment: our 34th president was told he did not have the right to access the base nor see what technology they had developed and/or uncovered through alien contacts.

Here's the point: I know this might sound like circular logic, but if UFOs are real, why would not the Dogman and Werewolf be so? Frankly, you'll read below at length about how "Victor," a US

---

[26] Citizen Hearing on Disclosure, "Deathbed Confession by Former CIA Agent on UFOs/The Anonymous Interview (Official Film Trailer)," YouTube, March 31, 2017. Retrieved 12/28/2020: https://www.youtube.com/watch?v=c--gGcsc4aw&feature=youtu.be.

Government agent, claims that they are - and that the US Government covers it up. Now, if the US Government would cover up their knowledge of UFOs, surely they would do the same thing with cryptids.

I might add here that where I reside in SoCal, San Bernardino County, there have been documented sightings of both Dogman[27] and Bigfoot[28] creatures. Talk about too close for comfort!

---

[27] See: Dogman Encounters Radio, "That's a Dogman! (Dogman Encounters Episode 211)," YouTube, August 3, 2018. Retrieved 12/28/2020: https://www.youtube.com/watch?v=2H4tZsUw62M; Mattsquatch Presents, "The Angeles Crest Dogman Encounter," YouTube, April 5, 2019. Retrieved 10/31/2020: https://www.youtube.com/watch?v=PuJDU8EIL0U.

[28] See Bigfoot Field Researchers Organization, Report #5160 ("Young Lady on Horseback Has a Face to Face Encounter One Late Afternoon"/October 25, 2002) and Report #6304 (Young Lady Believes the Creature is Back"/May 9, 2003).

<table>
<tr><td>WARNING...</td></tr>
<tr><td>

In closing, for this entire journey with you, whenever I reference and/or quote a source, it's going to be a small morsel of information - just a proverbial nibble - to entice you to take the time on your own and listen to the *entire source material.* Trust me. I know. You will not regret it.

</td></tr>
<tr><td>

FEAR APPROACHING!

</td></tr>
</table>

NOTES

CH II: HISTORY OF WEREWOLF

I must admit, when I first came across the notion that there was a "dogman" creature back in October of 2018 - which really exists according to various credible witnesses - I just assumed they were talking about what I was raised to think was a "werewolf." What I knew about the topic of Dogman/Werewolf was based upon my only exposure to said topic: *The Wolfman* film - my go to childhood source for horror: *Creature Features*. Well, that view is banal at best - and completely false - based upon what I know now.

After studying some of the various interviews of Victor the US Government agent tasked with hunting down errant cryptids (a podcast found on YouTube entitled *Dogman Encounters with Jeffrey Nadolny*), I realized how wrong I was on both accounts: Dogman exists, the Werewolf exists, they are two completely different cryptids, and they are real, flesh and blood creatures. So what is a Werewolf based upon the historical record?[29]

There are so many historical threads to the origins of the concept of the werewolf, be it the traditional supernatural understanding, or that the creature is real, it bleeds. The purpose below is not to create a comprehensive encyclopedic description of the history of the Werewolf, but rather to provide a basic sketch of same - to show you, the reader, the historical and cultural context of this alleged creature.

According to Wikipedia, which I always use as a starting point for any voluminous research, there is much to be learned about the Werewolf.

Of course, Ancient Egypt tops one of the earliest descriptions I can find on a werewolf. Anubis was their god of death, the afterlife, mummification, and the underworld, amongst other categories. He is

---

[29] Wikipedia: Werewolf.

normally depicted as a dog, or man with a dog's head, though as recently as 2015, it is more proper - due to DNA testing of the African Wolf commonly associated with this god - to indicate Anubis was a wolf.[30]

I find it highly significant that Anubis is by definition the protector of tombs, graves, and cemeteries, especially when considering that, of the four Linda Godfrey Variables of Native American Accoutrements (e.g. burial ground), Corn, Woods, and Water - burial grounds are one of them. In fact, many Dogman sightings are near cemeteries - or are they Werewolves mistaken for Dogmen?

The term and concept of a shapeshifting, supernatural werewolf dates back as early as Ancient Greece. Herodotus, perhaps the world's most famous historian, chronicled in his *Histories* (430 BC) the Neuri Tribe, which lived in what he called Scythia, an area centered around the Aral Sea in Southwest Russia today. He wrote

---

[30] Wikipedia: Anubis.

that this tribe transformed into wolves once a year for a few days.[31]

The concept of a "werewolf" clearly dates back to the Ancient Roman writer Petronius (27-66 AD) and his alleged novel *Satyricon*, which includes references to a werewolf. Note that this time period seems awful late in world history to see the first notion of this creature. Besides, as we will see below, the Werewolf is a living breathing creature and therefore, whether you believe in creationism or evolution or both, has to have been around as long as man has.

Most people would readily recognize the term and definition of a "werewolf" as a supernatural creature which involves "a human with the ability to shapeshift into a wolf (or, especially in modern film, a therianthropic hybrid wolf-like creature), either purposely or after being placed under a curse or affliction (often a bite or scratch from another werewolf) with the

____

[31] Wikipedia: Werewolf.

transformations occurring on the night of a full moon."[32]

It's interesting to note that the term "werewolf" is found in various languages throughout history. Is this literary prevalence proof that they exist? That werewolves are real? The following chart[33] identifies the etymology of various terms associated with the meaning of a werewolf viz-a-viz different cultures. Bear in mind that the actual definitions of each vary but tend to indicate the generalized concept thereof: a supernatural being which transforms from man to beast.

TERM	ETYMOLOGY
Garwalf	Anglo Norman
Gerulphus	Middle Latin
Kurtadam	Turkic Peoples of Central Asia

---

[32] Wikipedia: Werewolf.
[33] Ibid.

Kveldulf	Modern Scandinavian
Lycanthropy	Ancient Greek
Loup-garou	French
Varúlfur	Old Norse
Wariwulf	Old Frankish
Werwolf	Middle High German
Werehyena	Horn of Africa
Werejaguar	South America
Wereleopard	Asia
Werepuma	South America
Weretiger	India and Asia
Werewolf	Old English
Weriuuolf	Old High German

Ancient Greek and Roman literature has several werewolf-type accounts which have passed down through the ages. They appear to be fiction and nonfiction in nature. Worth further note is that the Roman Petronius' *Satyricon* (circa 60 AD) mentioned above included a storyline with a character who "stripped [naked] and piled his clothes by the roadside" and then turned into a werewolf.[34]

I find the description of the placement of the clothes fascinating. One modern source discussed at length below in a later chapter indicates that - when discovered in the wild - this is *definitely* a sign that a werewolf is present.[35] According to this eyewitness, the supernatural creature leaves his or her clothes near a trailhead or path, folded neatly for later use.

Along those same lines, the great St. Augustine, in his *The City of God* (early 400s AD), a deeply religious work, describes how witchcraft could be used to turn men

---

[34] Ibid.

[35] Dogman Encounters Radio, "My Uncles Killed a Dogman! (Dogman Encounters Episode 66)," YouTube, October 21, 2015. Retrieved 11/15/2020: https://www.youtube.com/watch?v=OXi6Umu6pWg.

into wolves; hence supernatural. Whether written as fiction or nonfiction, the fact that the many accounts described herein address the topic of werewolves indicates the level of awareness people had for these creatures - either supernatural or animal.

There are additional werewolf accounts worth examining briefly here. In Bordeaux, France (1603), a teen was actually accused of being a "werewolf."[36] Perhaps one of the most infamous accounts in world history of a series of gruesome werewolf attacks was the Beast of Gévaudan.[37] This creature or creatures, if that's what it was, killed some 100 men, women, and children (1764-1767), although a scientific study in 1987 estimated the death toll to be closer to 500 dead.

The terror which struck the countryside in Southern France was so strong that King Louis XV even offered financial assistance to some of the victims.

---

[36] Wikipedia: Werewolf.
[37] Wikipedia: Beast of Gévaudan.

Further, he ordered the French Government into the fray, hiring top hunters to track down the beasts. Several wolves were killed, two which were considered larger than normal. The last wolf was actually shot with a "silver bullet" on June 19, 1767.[38]

Though the modern printing press was not invented until circa 1440 in Germany by Johannes Gutenberg[39], fictional accounts of werewolves were told in print as early as the 12th Century, such as in the French poems or lais, *Bisclavret* and *Guillaume de Palerme*.[40] The former involves a man trapped as a werewolf by a sinister wife, and the latter involves a young couple who are saved by a werewolf. Werewolves have even been depicted in the media of the day such as woodcuts, one being by Lucas Cranach der Ältere, a German Renaissance painter, in 1512.[41]

---

[38] Ibid.
[39] Wikipedia: Printing Press.
[40] Wikipedia: Bisclavret and Guillaume de Palerme.
[41] Wikipedia: Werewolf.

With respect to other geographic areas, this belief in werewolves was and is widely held - and feared - in Europe starting in the Middle Ages and growing in significance from that time onward, culminating in "werewolf trials" starting in the 1400s, albeit small in number compared to those related to witchcraft.

This is not unusual if we consider that witchcraft was widely believed in and feared at this same time, and culminated in "witch trials" - perhaps the most famous being in Salem, Massachusetts, during the colonial period (February 1692-May 1693, a mere 72 years after the founding of the Plymouth Colony).

The earliest "werewolf trials" were in Switzerland of all places, but one of the more prominent ones was that of Peter Stumpp (1589). Known as the Werewolf of Bedburg (Western Germany), and after being tortured on the rack, Stumpp surprisingly admitted to quite a sinister resume. He was expert in black magic from the age of twelve thanks to Mephistopheles, from what Stumpp claimed, which allowed him to turn into a "greedy, devouring wolf, strong and mighty" with big eyes, mouth, teeth, body, and paws.[42]

With this dark power, Stumpp could roam the countryside and devour animals and people (14 kids, 2 pregnant women whose fetuses he tore from their wombs and "ate their hearts panting and raw"[43]). Reportedly, one of the kids was his own son and Stumpp ate his brain. Add to this, Peter Stumpp had an incestuous relationship with his daughter, a sexual relationship with a relative of some sort, and even succubus, an evil spirit which seeks male sperm to spawn demon children.[44]

For this, Stumpp, his daughter, and his relative were flayed (cut up), eventually killed, and their bodies burned. Interestingly, Stumpp's head was placed on public display alongside the figure of a wolf

---

[42] Wikipedia: Peter Stumpp.
[43] Ibid.
[44] Wikipedia: Succubus.

to discourage all who would follow his demonic path.[45] Apparently, the persecution of people accused of being a werewolf or "wolf charmer" occurred as late as the 1700s in Southern and Southeastern Austria.

During my research, I came across a lot of truly interesting facts. One that stood out was that one of the earliest *modern novels* about a werewolf was written by a woman, Clemence Annie Housman, *The Were-Wolf*, in 1896. Not only was Ms. Housman obviously a woman, but her main character was a *female* werewolf, and the story involved erotic fantasy no less.

Being a fan of *Unsolved Mysteries*, hosted principally by Robert Stack (1988-2002), an old TV show now airing on Netflix[46], I watched this show religiously and, with the miracles of reruns, have watched each episode at least twice. Some are obviously better than others.

---

[45] Wikipedia: Peter Stumpp.
[46] See Unsolved.com for the official website and Wikipedia: Unsolved Mysteries.

One particular episode, which deals with an area of Texas known as the Devil's Backbone, aired on December 15, 1995 (Season 8, Episode 8[47]). Located southwest of Austin about 30 miles (in the shape of a toy top, about 20 miles by 20 miles in length from its extremes), it is considered one of the most haunted natural areas in the country. Interestingly, prior to reviewing Josh Turner's research which is detailed below in a later chapter, I had watched this very episode (for the "umpteenth time") and then noted how Turner mentions this area and its connection to some of his research[48] just a fews days later.

But, what does this have to do with the topic of the Werewolf? Given that, by most accounts, the true definition of a Werewolf is one that states it is a supernatural being of

---

[47] Unsolved Mysteries, "Unsolved Mysteries with Robert Stack - Season 8 Episode 8 - Full Episode," March 4, 2019 (34:51-44:54). Retrieved 11/24/2020: https://www.youtube.com/watch?v=BnRZPr8omZg.

[48] Dogman Encounters Radio, "Dogman Encounters Episode 58," YouTube, September 2, 2015. Retrieved 11/21/2020: https://www.youtube.com/watch?v=A26lZtwyTBg.

sorts, a human that turns into this creature, this *Unsolved Mysteries* episode involves an eyewitness who claims to have been possessed by a - for lack of a better term - wolf's spirit while visiting a portion of the Devil's Backbone known as the Haunted Valley.

This eyewitness, John Villarreal, states that he was separated from his friends while exploring the area, spotted the spirit of a wolf above him on a rock outcropping, and that this spirit jumped into his body. Villarreal claims it possessed him. Feeling literally cold, as verified by his two friends as they drove him home, once there, the people present in the home claim that Villarreal went into some sort of trance and spoke about Native American History, particularly massacres perpetrated against them.[49]

---

[49] Unsolved Mysteries, "Unsolved Mysteries with Robert Stack - Season 8 Episode 8 - Full Episode," March 4, 2019 (41:13-43:58). Retrieved 11/24/2020: https://www.youtube.com/watch?v=BnRZPr8omZg.

To me anyway, as a serious Dogman researcher, the fact that Josh Turner mentions the Devil's Backbone, and in fact had visited it himself (albeit without any strange occurrences affecting him personally), gives credence to this supposed haunted site. Most importantly, it seems that Villarreal's account gives some support to the idea that a Werewolf is a supernatural or spiritual being.

An extremely important and wholeheartedly interesting piece of information stems from a *Dogman Encounters Radio* account, Episode 66.[50] The anonymous eyewitness from New Market, Alabama (henceforward dubbed "NM"), relays an interesting theory his uncles, who are professional hunters - and in fact hunted Dogman - told him about the origins of this creature. You see, they believe that Dogman could be a sort of shapeshifter,

---

[50] Dogman Encounters Radio, "My Uncles Killed a Dogman! (Dogman Encounters Episode 66)," YouTube, October 21, 2015 (40:15-41:25). Retrieved 11/15/2020: https://www.youtube.com/watch?v=QXi6Umu6pWg.

a human who becomes a werewolf or Dogman. (NM's account is discussed in detail in a later chapter below.)

Here's the kicker: NM's uncles told him that, if you ever find a set of cheap clothing (i.e. "from a thrift store") folded neatly on a rock, hanging in a bush or tree, or something along those lines, near a significant trail leading into the woods, *that is a sign of a werewolf.*[51] When the "creature" is done carousing, it will return, put on its clothes, and resume its life as a human. Mind boggling, but you have to consider the source: old timers, professional hunters, who know this creature, be it Werewolf or Dogman, through and through.

Juxtapose NM's accounting from his uncles of the origins of the Dogman with that of a Canadian man who happened to be homeless at the time of his encounter.[52] This account seems to show that this is a creature

---

[51] Ibid (48:28-49:35).
[52] Cryptids Canada, "Episode 123 Dogmen!!!! Will Eat You," YouTube, November 12, 2020. Retrieved: 11/20/2020: https://www.youtube.com/watch?v=0AsIIGsU5Xo.

of the most base and vile natural instincts of kill or be killed.

The Canadian eyewitness tells a typical homeless man's tale of being cold and trying to find a relatively warm, dry, and out of the way place to bunk for the night. He does not mince words. The Canadian bluntly states to the effect that Dogman is not a crock of bull. He adds that we are hors d'oeuvres for these creatures. Dogman, according to this Canadian, is extremely intelligent: "They know you're there long before you see them. If they aren't killing you, it's because they killed the idiot that was there before you."[53]

Bedding down inside the closet of an abandoned warehouse near the outskirts of town, this Canadian eyewitness found himself being hunted by a Dogman which was able to enter the building and find his location upstairs in the closet. Luckily, it had a dumbwaiter inside the closet, and the

---

[53] Ibid (1:45-1:55).

man was able to hide inside there and close the doors.

Though the Dogman repeatedly threw its body against the door, and made terrifying sounds, the Canadian man believed the isolation of his scent inside the steel dumbwaiter, coupled with the frustration caused by the Dogman's inability to get inside the closet[54], caused the creature to finally give up and leave. This man has no doubt that the Dogman would have killed him if it could have.[55]

The author of *Bayou Moon*, Jack LaFountain, recently discussed the basic distinctions[56] of a Werewolf, Loup-Garou (pronounced "loogaroo"), and Rougarou (pronounced "roo-ga-roo").[57]

---

[54] This is odd. By all accounts, Dogman has five fingers (with long nails) and can adroitly open doors and windows. I listened a couple of times to the account and no where does the Candian man describe how the creature tries to enter the closet. Did Dogman try to manipulate the door handle? Was the door locked? This Canadian eyewitness doesn't say.

[55] Ibid.

[56] Wiktionary: Loup-Garou. See also Wikipedia: Rougarou and Werewolf.

[57] Dogman Encounters Radio, "Dogman Encounters Episode 333 (Do You Believe in Werewolves?)," YouTube, November

Interestingly, LaFountain's hero contemplates the notion that, "There are no monsters. Man's the greatest monster that there is. But then he [LaFountain's hero] finds out over the course of the story that, yes, there are monsters, and this monster is . . . [a man]."[58] Wow! What an ironic rhetorical concept. Sure, it's nothing new, but the way LaFountain verbalizes it is profound.

This base idea reminds me of the Zodiac Killer and his enciphered remark (initial Three-Part Cipher sent on July 31, 1969, to three Bay Area newspapers[59]) that "man is the most dangerous animal of all," an idea which he undoubtedly borrowed from Richard Connell's strange book, *The Most Dangerous Game* (1924).[60]

20, 2020. Retrieved 11/20/2020: https://www.youtube.com/watch?v=SW1V9KTnrBU&feature=youtu.be.

[58] Ibid (8:33-8:48).

[59] For a tremendous website on the Zodiac Killer, see Tom Voigt's ZodiacKiller.com. Warning: You will spend a lot of time here - it's that interesting.

[60] Wikipedia: The Most Dangerous Game.

LaFountain's voice helps drive that terrible truth home.

LaFountain denotes the following denotative and cultural distinctions to the Werewolf, Loup-Garou, and Rougarou.[61]

WEREWOLF - A man who transforms into a beast like Lon Chaney, Jr.'s character in *The Wolfman* film (1941). It is a supernatural being.

LOUP-GAROU - A French term for a wolf (loup) and "man that becomes a beast" (garou). According to LaFountain, you become a Loup-Garou by being born one and then tasting human flesh or being bitten by one within the 101 days of the transformation period. This is the root word for "Rougarou."

ROUGAROU - This is a Cajun variation of the French term, "loup-garou." According to LaFountain, you become a Rougarou (he mistakenly states

---

[61] Dogman Encounters Radio, "Dogman Encounters Episode 333 (Do You Believe in Werewolves?)," YouTube, November 20, 2020 (15:54-17:54). Retrieved 11/20/2020: https://www.youtube.com/watch?v=SW1V9KTnrBU&feature=youtu.be.

"Loup-Garou" initially) by being born one and then tasting human flesh or being bitten by one within the 101 days of the transformation period.

He then lists some other chilling ways you can transform into a Rougarou: If you are the last person bitten during the 101 days of the transformation period; through a curse imposed by a witch or voodoo priestess; by revealing publicly who a Rougarou is; looking into the red eyes of a Rougarou; or for breaking Lent for seven years straight - in which case you will become a target of the Rougarou. (Wayward Catholics, take note!)

Though both a Werewolf and Rougarou are in effect "supernatural beings," LaFountain notes that a Rougarou can transform at will no matter the time of day - unlike a Werewolf which can only transform during a full moon or at night.

Also, whereas a Rougarou is typically a weak individual who transforms into a super-strong creature with only the heads and hands of a wolf, a Werewolf is an individual who transforms into a super-strong creature with the complete features of a wolf.

I assumed that, based upon my research and common sense that the Werewolf at least did not exist. And then, I came across another super source of information: *Dogman Encounters with Jeffrey Nadolny*. Founded on May 27, 2015, it currently has almost 4 million subscribers.

When I started this search for Dogman with you, I did not expect the journey to take this turn: an eyewitness named "William" - interviewed by Nadolny. (Note that in some episodes this most important eyewitness is called, "Victor.") I can only assume that he changed his real name to a pseudonym for privacy reasons. I state this because in one of the interviews the name "Bill" is used in reference to him; "Bill" is short for "William." It doesn't matter. The man deserves his privacy.

Henceforward, he will be referred to as "Victor."

Anyway, Victor's eyewitness testimony gets really interesting. I HIGHLY RECOMMEND that you listen to all of the *Dogman Encounters with Jeffrey Nadolny* interviews with Victor. (In one episode, Nadolny states that Victor participated in at least 50 interviews!)

He sounds like your grandpa telling you stories about his life. He's believable and honorable. Victor claims to have communicated with actual Werewolf creatures named Sebastian[62] and Rafael. The former told Victor that their history goes back to Ancient Egypt and India.[63]

---

[62] Dogman Encounters with Jeffrey Nadolny, "Dogman Gov't Agent William Shares More EP 44," YouTube, May 23, 2020. Retrieved 12/31/2020: https://www.youtube.com/watch?v=DG9kBd7MRx8.

[63] Dogman Encounters with Jeffrey Nadolny, "Dogman Subscriber Call-Ins with Victor Gov't Agent Part 3," YouTube, November 27, 2020 (33:53-34:21). Retrieved 11/28/2020: https://www.youtube.com/watch?v=WA0y8OIkls4.

Victor is a US Government intelligence agent (47 years) who hunts[64]/works with several cryptids including Bigfoot, Werewolves, and Dogman creatures (what Victor dubs the "Big Three"). He also claims to have gone on "black" or special ops with Werewolves - which included rescue missions of imprisoned Americans.

What is amazing to me is that Victor states the Werewolf is taught how to speak in the US breeding program with which he works. The "pups" learn somewhat from their mother and largely from an intercom system in the breeding program compound. The pups begin to speak around two years old.[65] Interestingly, Victor adds that the

---

[64] Dogman Encounters with Jeffrey Nadolny, "Dogman Gov't Agent William Shares More EP 44," YouTube, May 23, 2020 (47:54-49:09). Retrieved 12/31/2020: https://www.youtube.com/watch?v=DG9kBd7MRx8. Victor states that since he has started with the US Government Dogman and Werewolf Breeding Program, he has had to hunt down and kill the following wayward creatures over a thirty five year span: 875 Dogmen, 833 Werewolves, and 58 Bigfoot. He adds that agents get bonuses for killing same: $10,700 for Werewolf, $7,400 for Bigfoot, and $5,400 for Dogman.

[65] Dogman Encounters with Jeffrey Nadolny, "Dogman Gov't Agent William Shares More EP 44," YouTube, May 23, 2020

breeding program has never tried teaching the Werewolf a foreign language.[66]

With regards to the Dogman, Victor states that they cannot speak: "They can learn words - they can't speak it."[67] He clarifies that Dogman can understand words, and communicates physically through hand gestures and head nods, such as pointing to indicate where it wants to go, and nodding its head to affirm a "yes" answer to a question.

Victor reportedly works with various cryptids including Werewolves, Dogmen, Bigfoot (again, the "Big Three"), Vampires, and "super" Spiders, et al. He calls the Werewolf "my go to warriors."[68] I must admit, my understanding of the reasoning behind WHY the US Government and/or Military would want to use these creatures

____

(29:00-29:51). Retrieved 12/31/2020: https://www.youtube.com/watch?v=DG9kBd7MRx8.

[66] Ibid (31:40-31:51).

[67] Ibid (30:34-31:39).

[68] Dogman Encounters with Jeffrey Nadolny, "Dogman Subscriber Call-Ins with Victor Gov't Agent Part 3," YouTube, November 27, 2020 (26:05-26:10). Retrieved 11/28/2020: https://www.youtube.com/watch?v=WA0y8Qlkls4.

as soldiers appears logical, i.e. they are superior in strength, speed, etc., to a man or woman, but to release them into the wild is unfathomable for me.

As you will learn, Victor states that these creatures were promised their freedom upon the completion of x number of missions. You will also see that Victor believes that the Werewolf is a noble creature deserving of our love and respect for what they've done for our country, for you and me. At this point, I don't know what to think about that, however I do believe that Victor is absolutely real and credible.

Either way, through *Dogman Encounters with Jeffrey Nadolny*, Victor has offered up many hours of mindblowing eyewitness testimony.[69]

---

[69] These are only a partial accounting of the "William" or "Victor" interviews: Dogman Encounters with Jeffrey Nadolny, "Dogmen Gov't Agent Victor Communicates," YouTube, June 25, 2020. Retrieved 11/28/2020: https://www.youtube.com/watch?v=v5XRuPEmPKI [37:45]; Dogman Encounters with Jeffrey Nadolny, "Dogman Subscriber Call-Ins Q&A with Gov't Agent Victor]," YouTube, November 22, 2020. Retrieved 11/28/2020: https://www.youtube.com/watch?v=_3GOpXVprdE [Length

<table>
<tr><td colspan="2" align="center">Werewolf-Dogman Comparison Chart (Based Upon Eyewitness Victor's Account[70])</td></tr>
<tr><td>WEREWOLF (Average Full Grown Male)</td><td>DOGMAN (Average Full Grown Male)</td></tr>
<tr><td>Animal (Doesn't transform); most like a human,</td><td>Animal (German Shepherd looking); highly aggressive</td></tr>
</table>

1:41:35]; Dogman Encounters with Jeffrey Nadolny, "Dogman Subscriber Call-Ins Q&A with Gov't Agent Round 2," YouTube, November 25, 2020. Retrieved 11/28/2020: https://www.youtube.com/watch?v=MnQhPCYsmSI [Length 1:51:23]; Dogman Encounters with Jeffrey Nadolny, "Dogman Subscriber Call-Ins with Victor Gov't Agent Part 3," YouTube, November 27, 2020. Retrieved 11/28/2020: https://www.youtube.com/watch?v=WA0y8OlkIs4 [Length 1:54:23].

[70] This information comes largely from the following two interviews of "Victor": Dogman Encounters with Jeffrey Nadolny, "Dogman Subscriber Call-Ins Q&A with Gov't Agent Victor [Part 1]," YouTube, November 22, 2020 (1:08:28-1:11:38). Retrieved 11/28/2020: https://www.youtube.com/watch?v=_3GOpXVprdE; Dogman Encounters with Jeffrey Nadolny, "Dogman Victor (G Man) Does a 101 on the Big Three," YouTube, November 14, 2020 (3:20-13:39). Retrieved 12/1/2020: https://www.youtube.com/watch?v=n1UQnTB95us&t=3275s.

highly, highly intelligent; can communicate in English	
No tail	Tail (2-4 feet)
No muzzle [pronounced snout][71]; nose protrudes .5-.75 inches) and points up slightly	Muzzle (6-7 inches)
"Man with hair" presumably with human legs and "square face"; Body most like a human: V-shaped 34 inch waist (like a (bodybuilder), 58 inch chest, 24-26 inch arms (longer	Dog with human features and dog-like back legs (hocks); long neck

[71] Dogman Encounters with Jeffrey Nadolny, "Dogman Subscriber Call-Ins Q&A with Gov't Agent Round 2," YouTube, November 25, 2020 (52:39-52:55). Retrieved 11/28/2020: https://www.youtube.com/watch?v=MnQhPCYsmSI.

than a human); thick neck; thin hair on chest, cheeks, belly, thick hair on back of legs (6 inches long)	
Ears on side	Ears on top (pointed on top)
Can communicate in English	Can mimic language
Claws (1.75-2.75 inches); stout, can cut through ¼ inch plate steel	Claws (1.5-4 inches)
Height at maturity (7'10"-9 feet); Weight: I could not find a specific reference from Victor to the average weight. I can only assume that the Werewolf, which is more like a	Height at maturity (7.5-8 feet); Weight 350-500 lbs.

human, weighs typically less than a Dogman.	
Can run for 12 hours at 24-25 MPH[72]; Top speed of 45-48 MPH	Can run for 12 hours at 22 MPH; 1.5 hours at top speed of 35-40 MPH

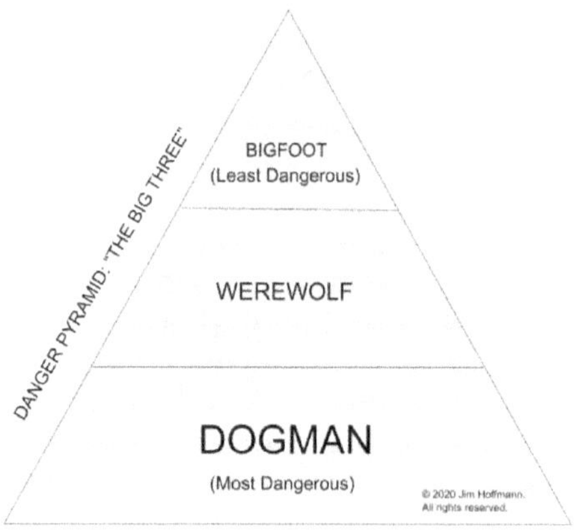

The entire issue of the Dogman and the Werewolf is still mind boggling. Unbelievable. The pure notion that I even

---

[72] Ibid.

entertain the thoughts thereof makes me think I'm either losing my mind or simply an intellectual simpleton. But, the evidence is too overwhelming. Everyone cannot be lying or making these stories up. I certainly do not think that *Dogman Encounters with Jeffrey Nadolny's* powerhouse guest, Victor, is fabricating anything.

My first impression of Victor[73] was one of incredulity, just like when I first heard *Dogman Encounters Radio* (Vic Cundiff) back in October 2018. No way! This can't be. I was discussing with my esteemed colleague this very question of "Do you

---

[73] Dogman Encounters with Jeffrey Nadolny, "Dogman Gov't Agent William Shares His Wyoming Encounter EP 20," YouTube, April 5, 2020. Retrieved 1/2/2021: https://www.youtube.com/watch?v=DFQG6Po_Kaw&feature= youtu.be. Wow! What a way to kick off a new year. Three werewolves actually save Victor's life. This is one of the most compelling, edge of my seat, eyewitness accounts I've ever heard. Jeffrey Nadolny's careful oral incantation of Victor's description of the hunt in Wyoming actually paints a humanitarian face on the soul of the Werewolf. His personal account is first and foremost unbelievable. Secondly, predicated upon Victor's wholehearted credibility, this account must be true. Since the Werewolf is the most intelligent of the Big Three, it makes sense that it is able to show compassion and empathy for fellow creatures - including humans.

believe in the Dogman and Werewolf or not?"

She listened to me intently and respectfully, yet I could see the aura of doubt cover her face when I described how Werewolves are highly intelligent creatures and can communicate with us. Remember that Victor states this to be true several times in his many interviews with Nadolny.

As a side note, I find it wholly ironic that, when you consider our recent election cycle, if Victor were a politician, the bulk of the population would immediately believe every word he says (evidence to the contrary be damned). Especially if his words were touted by one media source or another as the Gospel Truth. Politics aside, just sayin'....

So, is Victor legit? Is what he says credible? How can I - and ultimately you, the reader - determine this? Is it Victor's southern drawl which reminds me of my father-in-law who's Northern Alabaman through and through? Is it Victor's consistent and repetitive responses to these same or similar questions from different listeners over and over - never wavering, staggering, or stumbling from his original statements of fact? Or . . . is it a combination of all of the aforementioned factors?

Victor currently states that the US Government's Dogman and Werewolf breeding program centered in Virginia has been shut down. It's interesting that the reason for the shutdown of the former program is simply because they did not anticipate that the Dogman would naturally travel and congregate in packs. They do.

Victor also states that he and his team have seen packs as large as two hundred or so more or less take over towns. Pretty darn creepy if you ask me. The scientists were not able to remove that trait from the Dogman's psyche and social mores. The shutdown of the breeding program for the Dogman and Werewolf involves the "recalling" of the participants and their subsequent euthanization.[74]

One very strange eyewitness encounter which was within about 83 miles from my home involves a man named Jay in SoCal: Joshua Tree National Park in Twentynine Palms, California.[75] He was driving through the park late at night when it was technically closed. Apparently, at that time (circa 2010), the gates were open and the park rangers were not out patrolling the park after hours.

While driving south-southeast on Pinto Basin Road, Jay came across what he describes as a group of Dogmen in formation - marching: "I started seeing like a military group of animals that were three

____

[74] Dogman Encounters with Jeffrey Nadolny, "Dogman Gov't Agent: The Answers are Finally Getting Answered," YouTube, October 10, 2020 (4:40-8:17). Retrieved 12/1/2020: https://www.youtube.com/watch?v=BmPEWXo1QJg&feature=youtu.be.

[75] Dogman Encounters Radio, "Dogman Encounters Episode 335 (The Dogmen Were Walking in Formation)," YouTube, December 4, 2020. Retrieved 12/4/2020: https://www.youtube.com/watch?v=YF9VY76ujQU&feature=youtu.be.

rows wide and about four rows deep."[76] My first reaction upon hearing this statement, having just studied Victor's comparison of the Dogman and Werewolf, was that the group was most definitely Werewolves.

But what makes this a strange encounter? Jay describes the following characteristics of the creatures he saw that night, which I compared to Victor's descriptions above in the Werewolf-Dogman Comparison Chart: wide head, no neck (Werewolf), mane of hair, hair to top of shoulder blades, dog legs or hocks (Dogman), 2.5 foot tail (Dogman), and large ears off to the side (Werewolf).[77]

I don't know, but it seems like Jay described a combination Werewolf-Dogman creature. The characteristics of having no neck or a thick neck (Dogman has a long neck), and ears off to the side of the head (Dogman has ears that are pointed on top),

---

[76] Ibid (19:48-20:02).
[77] Ibid (32:27-33:00).

makes we wonder what Jay really saw that night.

With all due respect to the eyewitness, eyewitnesses are notorious for being wrong. It's that simple. Unless there is some sort of hybrid Werewolf-Dogman creature which has features of both a Werewolf (i.e. no neck and large ears off to the side and a Dogman (i.e. dog legs or hocks and a 2.5 foot tail), then we can only assume that Jay - who seems pretty rational and precise - garbled some of the characteristics. For me, when he stated "tail" - that was the clincher. I find it hard to imagine getting that characteristic wrong.

After examining all of the evidence available to me, it is doubtful that all werewolf encounters are shapeshifters, rougarou, etc. Contrariwise, I do think the evidence shows that they are also - if not primarily - God's and nature's creation.

Victor the Government Agent Addict? Additional Known Sources
Dogman Encounters with Jeffrey Nadolny, "Dogman Gov't Agent William Speaks Out Part 2 EP 42," YouTube, May 15, 2020. Retrieved 12/5/2020: https://www.youtube.com/watch?v=_yC Sw6CS10 (1:03:27).
Dogman Encounters with Jeffrey Nadolny, "Dogman Gov't Agent Speaks About Hunts and Answers More Questions EP 43," YouTube, May 17, 2020. Retrieved 12/5/2020: https://www.youtube.com/watch?v=aSp5 wv3Lfgo (57:10).

Dogman Encounters with Jeffrey Nadolny, "Dogman Gov't Agent William Shares More EP 44," YouTube, May 23, 2020. Retrieved 12/5/2020: https://www.youtube.com/watch?v=DG9kBd7MRx8 (58:54).

NOTES

CH III: HISTORY OF DOGMAN

Again, my exposure to the entire topic of Dogman was superficial and limited to my understanding of Lon Chaney, Jr.'s portrayal of a werewolf in the classic horror flick, *The Wolf Man*. Note that, until October of 2018, I had no idea Dogman even existed. Admittedly, after all of my research, I'm still trying to ascertain the origins and purpose of a Werewolf and a Dogman? On the other hand, how are we to judge the value of anything be it a dinosaur or an amoeba? Only God - or Mother Nature if you prefer - knows . . . if you follow my meaning. Hence, why do I exist? Why do you exist?

Again, according to Wikipedia, in the fifth century BC, the Greek physician Ctesias, in his *Indica*, wrote a detailed report on the existence of cynocephali in India.[78]

Similarly, the Greek traveller Megasthenes (circa 350 to 290 BC) who wrote *Indica*, a "travel guide" of sorts about India, claimed to know about dog-headed people in India who lived in the mountains, communicated through barking, wore the skins of wild animals, and lived by hunting.

The original historian, Herodotus (circa 484 to 425 BC), dubbed the "Father of History" by Cicero himself, reports claims by ancient Libyans that such creatures inhabited the east of their lands, as well as that of headless men and various other anomalies. Now, that's weird. However, I can understand that the level of credibility was probably based less on what could be scientifically proven and more upon what someone was willing to merely believe. Yet, since I am seriously researching and writing about "dogman" and "werewolf" creatures, I will refrain from criticizing any strange

---

[78] Wikipedia: Cynocephaly.

accounts, cryptid or otherwise, including those of headless men.

One shocking find of this research was incomprehensible. The German bishop and poet Walter of Speyer portrayed St. Christopher as a giant of a cynocephalic species in the land of the Chananeans (Canaan in the New Testament) who ate human flesh and barked.[79] According to tradition, eventually Christopher met the Christ child, regretted his former behavior, and received baptism.

He was rewarded with a human appearance, whereupon he devoted his life to Christian service and became an Athleta Christi, one of the military saints. Throughout history, Christopher was sometimes pictured with a dog's head but that icon or notion of the saint is generally not supported by the Catholic Church (Roman or Eastern Orthodox); definitely

---

[79] Ibid.

strange. Further, the homage paid to him has waned over the years.[80]

The renowned Muslim researcher and scholar and world traveller, Ibn Battuta, encountered what were described as "dog-mouthed" people on his journey, possibly describing a group of Mentawai people who practice teeth sharpening, and who live on an island between India and Sumatra.

Ibn Battuta notes: "Fifteen days after leaving Sunaridwan we reached the country of the Barahnakar, whose mouths are like those of dogs. This tribe is a rabble, professing neither the religion of the Hindus nor any other. They live in reed huts roofed with grasses on the seashore, and have abundant banana, areca, and betel trees. Their men are shaped like ourselves, except

---

[80] McDonald, Thomas L., "The Strange Legend of St. Christopher, and Whether or Not He Had the Head of a Dog," WeirdCatholic.com, August 10, 2018. Retrieved 1/28/2021: https://weirdcatholic.com/2018/08/10/the-strange-legend-of-st-christopher-and-whether-or-not-he-had-the-head-of-a-dog/.

that their mouths are shaped like those of dogs....”[81]

In Charlemagne's court (aka Charles the Great, circa 742-814 AD, the first Holy Roman Emperor), the Norse were given this attribution, implying un-Christian and less-than-human qualities: "I am greatly saddened" said the King of the Franks in Notker the Stammerer's well-noted documentation of the emperor's life,[82] "that I have not been thought worthy to let my Christian hand sport with these dog-heads."[83]

The thirteenth-century encyclopedist Vincent of Beauvais acquainted his patron Saint Louis IX of France with "an animal with the head of the dog but with all other members of human appearance... Though he behaves like a man... and, when peaceful, he is tender like a man, when furious, he becomes cruel and retaliates on humankind. The list of, dare I say, reputable references

---

[81] Ibid.
[82] Wikipedia: Notker the Stammerer.
[83] Wikipedia: Cynocephaly.

in history to a Dogman continues unabated...[84]

The epic Anglo-Saxon poem, *Beowulf* (975-1025), describes a half-dog;

The old Welsh poem, *Pa Gur* (13th Century), describes "dog heads";

Italian traveller and diplomat Giovanni da Pian del Carpine (1185-1252), who visited the Court of the Great Khan, describes how Ögedei Khan encountered "a race of dog heads" near Lake Baikal in Southern Russia;

Marco Polo (1254-1324), in his *The Travels of Marco Polo*, describes "dog-headed barbarians" who are cruel and look like Mastiffs. Interestingly, Polo travelled between 1271-1295, and a romance writer, Rustichello da Pisa, wrote the book, published circa 1300. But, by all accounts, *The Travels* became a best seller of sorts;

The Chinese Buddhist missionary, Hui Shen or Hoei-Shin (5th Century), in the *Book of Liang* (635 AD), describes

____

[84] Ibid.

dog-headed people in either Japan or the Americas after returning from a 20,000 mile voyage in 499 AD.[85] They called the place in the Americas, Fusang;[86]

And the various descriptions and accountings of Dogman go on and on.

Fast forward to 1887, Wexford County in Northwest Michigan, USA. This was perhaps *the first recorded* Dogman sighting in America.[87] Reportedly, two loggers spotted a creature with the physical makeup of a man but with a dog's head. As I note in this work, Michigan - without a doubt - is a highly active place for Dogman (and perhaps Werewolf) encounters.

The author (Lyra Radford) of this excellent article graciously includes a

---

[85] For an interesting look at the idea that the Chinese - Buddhist monks no less - actually discovered America one thousand years before Columbus, check out the controversial book by Charles Michael Boland, *They All Discovered America*, Doubleday, 1961.

[86] Wikipedia: Fusang.

[87] Radford, Lyra, "12 Darkly Fascinating Stories of the Michigan Dogman," Ranker.com, January 3, 2020. Retrieved 12/23/2020:
https://www.ranker.com/list/dogman-stories/lyra-radford.

recording which I had been searching for but lost - until now. Though it is not for the faint of heart, I HIGHLY RECOMMEND you listen to this extremely creepy recording[88] of an alleged Dogman or Werewolf attack on a Michigan couple. I must admit, the recording has an air of fiction to it.

Since my wife swears by OnStar, I'm familiar with how it works. I'm not sure why the call would be dropped after the alleged creature attacks the couple. Though the call is placed with a cell phone, the call is then modulated by the dashboard computer and not the cell phone per se . . . unless the alleged victim herein inadvertently disconnected the call for whatever reason. I hate to think that I could be wrong. My God, what these poor people would have experienced - if real.

As I also note in this work, Wisconsin - without a doubt - is a highly active place

---

[88] ShifterMythology, "Michigan Dogman/Werewolf Attack 911 Call (Real Recording/Audio Footage)," May 27, 2012. Retrieved 12/23/2020: https://www.youtube.com/watch?v=jZCSc0ned3Q&feature=emb_title.

for Dogman (and Werewolf) encounters, too. Perhaps the most famous is the Beast of Bray Road, which Linda Godfrey documents in her book of the same name, mentioned above.

Yet, the most gruesome account appears to be that of the famous LBL Case. Interestingly, Victor claims the infamous Land Between the Lakes Dogman attack [February-March 1982[89]], where a family was literally mutilated, with arms and legs thrown into nearby trees[90], was perpetrated by wild Werewolves (which he claims were

---

[89] Bigfoot Crossroads, "The Dogman of LBL Bigfoot Outlaw Radio EP 40 Part 3," YouTube, November 2, 2017 (00:35-1:00). Retrieved 12/10/2020: https://www.youtube.com/watch?v=DnRxX-qCUtY. Frankly, this story is riveting. The storyteller (Tim Coonbo Baker) adds that the father was dismembered and decapitated, and that the daughter was found partially eaten. It's interesting to note, however, that Victor clearly states in his accounts that the creature was a Werewolf and not a Dogman. Furthermore, Victor states that the metal camper trailer was torn open and that that (strong claws/nails which can tear through ¼ inch steel) is a characteristic of a Werewolf.

[90] Fandom, "Beast of the Land Between the Lakes," Cryptidz.Fandom.com, Date Unknown. Retrieved 11/29/2020: https://cryptidz.fandom.com/wiki/Beast_of_the_Land_Between_the_Lakes.

not part of the US Military program) *and obviously not Dogmen.*[91]

In a separate interview[92], Victor states that his father actually worked the case. He describes what witnesses told his father: People near the camper trailer which was attacked claimed they heard the standard "silence" of the forest which normally occurs when large predators are in the area particularly a Dogman or Werewolf. After a time, the standard noises of crickets and birds returned.

Suddenly, sometime in the late evening, the witnesses heard an "explosion," "screaming," "metal ripping," and that after about "60 seconds - everything stopped." The witnesses called the local authorities and Victor states that they found the family

---

[91] Dogman Encounters with Jeffrey Nadolny, "Dogman Subscriber Call-Ins Q&A with Gov't Agent Round 2," YouTube, November 25, 2020 (1:19:14-1:19:53). Retrieved 11/28/2020: https://www.youtube.com/watch?v=MnQhPCYsmSI.

[92] Dogman Encounters with Jeffrie Nadolny, "Dogman Victor Shares His Father's and His Similar Hunts," YouTube, November 19, 2020 (5:17-12:06). Retrieved 12/10/2020: https://www.youtube.com/watch?v=i7S-kWrxXLE.

dead: the father near the front door of the camper trailer - as if he was trying to escape, the mother "destroyed inside the trailer" [I even read one incredible account that claimed she was raped, although that seems too far fetched.], the young son 30 feet behind the trailer, and the young daughter's remains two miles away in a tree.

Victor states that his father told him, the coroner believed the attacks were due to a mountain lion or a bear. DNR (Department of Natural Resources) was then called in to investigate and determined - based upon the literally torn metal siding of the camper trailer - that it could *not* have been a bear or mountain lion. (Again, remember that Victor states that Werewolves have powerful nails/claws (1.75-2.75 inches) which can rip through one quarter inch plate steel.)

At this point, Victor's father was called in to investigate. In fact, Victor states his father found the tracks to the creature. Later that night, he hunted the creature with a member of his team, sort of a Men in Black for Cryptids (my words). Sadly, the two hunters found the girl's remains, blood dripping down as if to beckon them . . . "Here I am. Here is all that remains."

Victor's father shrewdly chose to start the hunt from the tree where the remains were discovered. The next day, late in the evening, they lie in wait for the creature. It came back to the same tree with Victor's father at the ready, and he "took it out - and that was a Werewolf."[93]

Dogman Narratives is another really cool source where the topic of discussion is pretty eclectic, from UFOs to the bizarre (Japanese Doll Village of Nagoro), to Cryptids, including Dogman. Founded on March 10, 2017, the channel has 7.5K subscribers and 900K views. Their presentation of the topic at hand generally involves a very professional animated presentation. In fact, they created an awesome animated video related to this

---

[93] Ibid (11:58-12:02).

so-called Beast of LBL, though it relates to a different case.[94]

---

[94] Dogman Narratives, "Land Between the Lakes - Beast of LBL (Dogman Narratives Episode 5)," YouTube, September 1, 2017. Retrieved 11/29/2020: https://www.youtube.com/watch?v=9Ottm19-xMg.

CH IV: THE DOGMAN

The simple definition of a Dogman, *based upon my research*, as an animal or creature (By this I mean natural and not spiritual, although some believe the latter to be the case.) that looks like a dog or wolf, but can stand like a human. In fact, they are known to be extremely fast on four legs as well as two.

What does a typical Dogman look like? I admit that there are so many different descriptions of what these creatures look like. (Some believe they can even look like a Bigfoot.) It's generally believed amongst Dogman aficionados that there are seven known types.

Although my research has not focused on this aspect of the Dogman creature, and most accounts I've studied involve what I would describe as a typical Dogman ("werewolf" or Van Helsing-like), according to Mattsquatch Presents[95], these are the seven known types: 1) Baboon-like; 2) Chow-like; 3) Sasquatch-like; 4) Timber Wolf-like; 5) Hyena-like; 6) Van Helsing-like; 7) Soldier-like. Interestingly, the last type reminds me of - for whatever reason - Scar's sidekicks in the classic Disney film, *The Lion King*.[96] You remember, if you have kids in their 20s and 30s, Shenzi, Banzai, and Ed. I know, but they are hyenas, right? Google the images thereof and make up your own mind. Just sayin'.

It's striking how most accounts involve a Dogman creature with legs *like a dog*, which is what one would expect to see - specifically the hock or inverted angle at the mid-portion of the hind legs at the junction of what would be the knee. Yet, there are

---

[95] Mattsquatch Presents, "The Seven Types of Dogmen," YouTube, March 7, 2018. Retrieved November 7, 2020: https://www.youtube.com/watch?v=OZKts7G-gkg&feature=youtu.be. See also Mattsquatch Presents, "The Dogman Cometh," YouTube, November 10, 2020. Retrieved 11/10/2020: https://www.youtube.com/watch?v=TO8l3DOKmlo.

[96] Wikipedia: Scar (The Lion King).

also accounts of the Dogman creature with legs *like a human*, in other words no hock, and with relatively similar proportion and morphology thereto. Mattsquatch Presents states in fact that of the aforementioned seven known types of Dogman, types 1-3 have legs like a human, and 4-7 have legs like a dog.[97]

I personally have no clue as to the veracity of this information. However *Mattsquatch Presents*[98] does depict quite clearly that these creatures either have hind legs that are bent like a dog's, or are similar in structure to that of a human.[99] That is a key characteristic to me, and very interesting. But it gets better.

Naturally, Dogman has a dog-like head, with ears pointing typically up like a

---

[97] Mattsquatch Presents, "The Dogman Cometh," YouTube, November 10, 2020. Retrieved 11/10/2020: https://www.youtube.com/watch?v=TO8I3DOKmlo.

[98] Mattsquatch Presents, "The Seven Types of Dogmen," YouTube, March 7, 2018. Retrieved November 7, 2020: https://www.youtube.com/watch?v=OZKts7G-gkg&feature=youtu.be.

[99] Check out DER Episodes 211 and 268 for accounts where the witness saw a Dogman creature with human legs.

dog's, and sometimes tufts of hair sticking skyward. They also typically have some sort of snout, although the structure and length varies from short to long. But, the Dogman also invariably has hands and fingers like a human. Most accounts describe the creature as having some sort of tail. Many are extremely agile and strong. Most are aggressive and extremely intelligent.

The bottom line? The descriptions of the eyewitnesses vary to some degree across the spectrum, but most if not all are wolf or dog-like in appearance, can stand on two legs, and should be considered dangerous in most - if not all - instances.

One of the absolute best eyewitness descriptions of a Dogman encounter, in my humble opinion, is that of Brandon Close[100] in Cato, New York. I have listened to this account several times. It's that engrossing. This episode of DER is a must listen. A

---

[100] Dogman Encounters Radio, "That was a Werewolf! (Dogman Encounters Episode 190)," YouTube, March 2, 2018. Retrieved 11/8/2020: https://www.youtube.com/watch?v=5ms-q2jpMeo.

young man in his thirties at the time, Close lived on a 192 acre farm with his wife and daughter. The area is rural and surrounded by large swaths of forest.

On Friday, February 2, 2018, Close's wife noticed his cattle were behaving strangely. They gathered shoulder to shoulder at one point in their corral, farthest away from the tree line. Furthermore, their dog would not go outside. Close initially assumed it was a wolf pack. Once he returned home from work that night, he heard a strange "blood curdling howl" - not once but twice. This noise made the cattle exceptionally nervous.

Close asked his friend to help him eradicate the problem that night, and the two, armed, went searching for a wolf. What they saw was indescribable.

A few minutes from his home, enroute in a Razor buggy, he and his neighbor drove down a dark dirt road and were approached by several deer running towards them and then past them....

DOGMAN CHARACTERISTICS Brandon Close Account[101] (Circa 24:00-49:00)	
HEIGHT	8-9 feet tall, looks a lot like *Van Helsing* werewolf (viewed from 15-18 feet away)
INTE-LECT	Menacing, cunning (toyed with them by slowing down vehicle with right arm and smiling at them), stealthy (tried to flank Brandon and friend), understood threat of gun (ducked when firearm pointed at it)
HEAD	Huge
FUR	Moderate length, skin visible
SNOUT	Long, dog-like, razor sharp teeth

---

[101] Dogman Encounters Radio, "That was a Werewolf! (Dogman Encounters Episode 190)," YouTube, March 2, 2018. Retrieved 11/8/2020: https://www.youtube.com/watch?v=5ms-q2jpMeo.

EARS	Pointed (8-10 inches)
EYES	Bright, yellow gold - like Corona beer[102][103]
ARMS	Normal human length above elbows, extra long below elbows, powerful and muscular
HANDS	Five fingers with long black nails like "black knives"
TORSO	Buff chest, abs, narrow waist, when shot in pecs no effect (875 Remington Pump with brass shells)
LEGS	Fast, powerful (knocked over

[102] Dogman Encounters Radio, "Dogman Encounters Episode 51," YouTube, July 15, 2015 (32:34-33:08). Retrieved 11/26/2020: https://www.youtube.com/watch?v=dt0EI0oQ8Ok. On Thanksgiving night 2020, I was struck by DER 51 guest Adam Davis' opinion on the eyeshine of a Dogman. He notes that some he has seen have red eyes, some yellow. Davis speculates that, like the Box Turtle, where males have red eyes and females have brown eyes, Dogman males may have red and females yellow.

[103] Dogman Encounters Radio, "Dogman Encounters Episode 268 (Boss Dogman!)," YouTube, September 6, 2019. In Northeast Riverside County (SoCal), not too far from where I live, "Brad" saw a definite male with yellow eyes in June of 2019 (25:00-25:05).

	trees while running), runs 50 mph on two legs at no greater than a 45 degree angle, loud cracking noise (bones cracking) as it stood up, back legs like a dog (hocks), jumped 15 feet up into tree and 30 feet across dirt road
TAIL	Not described

Another excellent eyewitness description of a Dogman encounter is that of Larry Parker, a Vietnam Vet and former member of a Marine recon unit.[104] This account originates out of northern Michigan which is close to ground zero for the Dogman phenomenon. In other words, Michigan has had some of the earliest known encounters of this creature in America dating back many years to 1887.[105] I

---

[104] Dogman Encounters Radio, "I Shot a Dogman with a .30-06 Rifle! (Dogman Encounters Episode 21)," YouTube, February 17, 2015. Retrieved 11/9/2020: https://www.youtube.com/watch?v=YlVn-GJJxYk&t=1417s.

[105] Encyclopaedia of Cryptozoology, "Michigan Dogman," CryptidArchives.Fandom.com, Date Unknown. Retrieved

have listened to Larry Parker's account several times.

The area is obviously rural and surrounded by large swaths of forest. Interestingly, Parker emphasizes to all that will heed his warning that Dogman is not to be hunted, antagonized, threatened in any way. He states to "leave it alone." Dogman can be shot with a serious round and still attack as if struck by nothing. If someone seeks to do this, for whatever reason, Parker believes it will not end well for the pursuers. The hunters, with Dogman, will become the hunted.

DOGMAN CHARACTERISTICS Larry Parker Account[106] (Circa 44:42-47:40)	
HEIGHT	7-7.5 feet tall

11/9/2020:
https://cryptidarchives.fandom.com/wiki/Michigan_Dogman.
[106] Dogman Encounters Radio, "I Shot a Dogman with a .30-06 Rifle! (Dogman Encounters Episode 21)," YouTube, February 17, 2015. Retrieved 11/9/2020:
https://www.youtube.com/watch?v=YIVn-GJJxYk&t=1417s.

INTE-LECT	Could have run him down but not interested in him, rather interested in his friend who lived nearby
HEAD	Not described
FUR	Hairy
SNOUT	Freakish growl
EARS	Not described
EYES	Not described
ARMS	Similar to human
HANDS	Claws
TORSO	Chest a combination of human and dog, rounded shoulders (like a bear)
LEGS	Front similar to human, but thighs "narrowed down" at ankle area, foot did not match human, and back legs had hocks like a dog

TAIL	Not described

A third excellent eyewitness description of a Dogman encounter is that of "John," a veteran, ex-CIA, proficient in firearms - and his wife.[107] This DER guest has had so many encounters in his Ohio home that he can be heard on DER Episodes 233 (Part 1) and (Part 2) and 234.

Since this account originates out of Ohio, it is also close to ground zero for the Dogman - and Bigfoot - phenomenon. In other words, Ohio is teeming with Dogman *and* Bigfoot encounters. I have listened to John's accounts many times over. Frankly, he is an excellent storyteller and eyewitness.

---

[107] Dogman Encounters Radio, "Dogman Encounters Episode 233 (Part 1) (A 1,000 Pound Dogman!)," YouTube, January 4, 2019. Retrieved 11/11/2020: https://www.youtube.com/watch?v=AyPVMHdfl6E&t=7s. Dogman Encounters Radio, "Dogman Encounters Episode 233 (A 1,000 Pound Dogman! (Part 2)," YouTube, January 11, 2019. Retrieved 11/11/2020: https://www.youtube.com/watch?v=bmY0Y1AzStc. Dogman Encounters Radio, "Dogman Encounters Episode 234 (A 1,000 Pound Dogman! (Bonus Episode)," YouTube, January 13, 2019. Retrieved 11/11/2020: https://www.youtube.com/watch?v=-AbOXjJC-mo.

The area is obviously rural and surrounded by large swaths of forest.

I must say, this man's calmness when describing his interactions gives me some hope that not all Dogman encounters have to be bad. John comes across as accepting the fact that he has to live with the creatures, along with several Bigfoot, and is OK with it. John does admit to DER host Vic Cundiff in Episode 234 that he'd prefer not to have to deal with either Bigfoot or Dogman, although he's not really afraid of the former. In other words, John stated that if he never saw either one again, he'd be perfectly fine with that.

The operative word of description for John is "brave." John admits in Episode 234 that he's not really afraid of Bigfoot (he states they're "shy"), but he is afraid of Dogman. In Episode 233 (Part 2), he states matter-of-factly that Dogman is "sneaky."

DOGMAN CHARACTERISTICS

"John's" Account[108] (Circa 29:11-48:45)	
HEIGHT	7 feet
INTE-LECT	Surprised look, then sneer, scowl
HEAD	Chow-type (like a dandelion with a dogface) with hair sticking straight up, three-times larger than normal proportion to body size (unnatural looking)
FUR	Smokey gray, 6-8 inches long near top, thick around shoulders and neck, but tapers off down toward bottom of body, "mane like a lion" and "well-groomed"
SNOUT	Very red, 4-5 inches long, black fur, extremely sharp teeth (like a wood rasp), "pearly white

108 Dogman Encounters Radio, "Dogman Encounters Episode 233 (Part 1) (A 1,000 Pound Dogman!)," YouTube, January 4, 2019. Retrieved 11/11/2020: https://www.youtube.com/watch?v=AyPVMHdfl6E&t=7s.

	half inch long" with multiple rows, 4 canines of 1.5-2 inches in length
EARS	Not described
EYES	Black
ARMS	Human-like, short hair on arms, light skinned
HANDS	Not described
TORSO	Skinny, looked "malnourished," abs bodybuilder-like, rest of body human-like, light skinned
LEGS	Human-like
TAIL	Not described

John has had the fortune *or misfortune* of living within a "cryptid range" of Dogman and Bigfoot. Through his varied encounters, John has been able to generally describe the unique behaviors of each. It's quite interesting to compare John's commentary[109] about both cryptids.

DOGMAN BEHAVIORS	BIGFOOT BEHAVIORS
Chow-type curious about him, not as aggressive	When aggravated, will through rocks at the house, "smack" the side of the house
Canine-type "very aggressive and sinister," not afraid to "hold their ground"	Aggressive if need be, if let alone and respected will "come to terms" with humans[110]
Canine-type strategic and	Tend to be protective of

---

[109] Taken from John's Dogman Encounters Radio interviews, Parts 1 and 2 (Episode 233) and the Bonus Episode (Episode 234).

[110] I heard a few accounts involving scrapes between Dogman and Bigfoot. In one account, a Bigfoot family is eviscerated by two Dogmen. See Cryptid Canada, ""Episode 109 Dogmen Killed a Family of Bigfoot," YouTube, October 13, 2020. Retrieved 11/22, 2020: https://www.youtube.com/watch?v=_-rfVnBiEo8.

tactical and will direct your attention elsewhere (in cahoots with other Dogman creatures) and outflank you	humans through warnings of Dogman's presence
Canine-type chased Bigfoot away	Biceps as big as John's waist, strong though not necessarily "buff"
Birds and insects silent in Dogman's presence	Methodical in their migration to and fro: will disappear for 10-12 days then come back for 2-3 days and repeat the process
Roar, bark, once two Dogmen working in tandem on either side of John used a little girl's voice to cry out, "Help Me! Help	Scream

<table>
<tr><td>Me!"</td><td></td></tr>
</table>

Now, my favorite eyewitness account of all time, *Dogman Encounters Radio* or otherwise, is Episode 66 of DER.[111] A young man, who works in the emergency room of a nearby hospital, recounts his experience with his uncles who apparently hunted cryptids for money to rid people of these living nightmares.

I highly, highly recommend everyone and anyone interested in this topic listen to this anonymous eyewitness - from small town New Market in northern Alabama - discuss the Dogman phenomenon. This account is riveting. I will call him "NM."

Not only does NM describe what he personally saw and experienced, but he actually *did his own research* and shares his uncle's unique views on the origins and characteristics of Dogman.

---

[111] Dogman Encounters Radio, "My Uncles Killed a Dogman! (Dogman Encounters Episode 66)," YouTube, October 21, 2015. Retrieved 11/15/2020: https://www.youtube.com/watch?v=OXi6Umu6pWg.

Interestingly, NM notes that his uncles describe three key cryptids which they've encountered: 1) Sasquatch or Bigfoot; 2) Bearfoot or Bearsquatch (a creature with the body of a Bigfoot but the head of a bear); 3) Dogman. I find it extremely interesting yet not surprising that the NM states that his uncles believe that Bearfoot and Dogman are the most dangerous.[112]

NM goes on to describe many more significant yet equally horrifying "facts" as parlayed to him by his prudent uncles. They told NM that Dogman was "too hard to kill" and that "you have to be able to run 'em down somewhere."[113] This makes sense. By all accounts that I've read, the Dogman is extremely intelligent and almost *impossible* to kill even with high powered rifles. In fact, this is the only eyewitness account I've read that describes the actual killing of one of these creatures.

____

[112] Ibid (3:45-4:17).
[113] Ibid (4:58-5:19).

In chilling fashion, NM describes how his uncles, with apparent earnestness, told him that the "Dogman liked to make people disappear."[114] For example, they might purposefully cross a road in front of an oncoming vehicle, forcing someone to drive off of the road, and then grab that individual - who'd never be seen again.

Or, if someone sleeps with an open window or door, Dogman will oblige and creep inside or simply reach through the window, grab the unsuspecting victim by the leg, and pull that frightened prey straight outside and into oblivion. If the victim had a large porch, NM's uncles stated another trick of the creature would be to get the individual to come outside while the Dogman was perched on the porch above the door, ready to snatch the unsuspecting individual upwards to their death.[115]

Yes, Dogman, as my title suggests, is nature's scariest cryptid for a lot of reasons.

---

[114] Ibid (5:42-7:49).
[115] Ibid.

NM's uncles paint a gruesome picture with respect to how the Dogman removes human body parts, including heads, and scatters them in trees and bushes as a form of warning to all who beckon to invade their territory. Thankfully, according to the uncles, this ferocious creature does not *eat humans*. Not sure if that makes me feel any bit better about this creature.[116]

One of the reasons why I chose to write a book about Dogman is the overwhelming fact that they are absolutely fearless, almost indestructible, and perhaps most haunting, extremely intelligent. In fact, NM tells how his uncles did not relish having to hunt Dogman for the reasons heretofore described: "If they [Dogman] get where they know you're after 'em, then you pretty much gotta quit."[117]

NM adds something quite chilling which I've heard and or read about a few times. Apparently, Dogman has the ability

---

[116] Ibid (8:15-9:32).
[117] Ibid (12:42-12:48).

to speak English, or at least enunciate expressions or sounds like a "crying baby" or "screaming woman."[118]

The pinnacle of this interview comes when NM describes his actual interface with a dead Dogman, killed by his savvy uncles, apparently hired to rid a homeowner of this menacing creature. Again, I recommend you listen to this episode of DER. For the purposes of this story, I want to detail what NM saw.

DOGMAN CHARACTERISTICS "NM's Account"[119] (Circa 22:35-28:50)	
HEIGHT	Tall
INTE-LECT	Extremely hard to catch and it took several shotgun blasts to kill it, high pitched scream that could shatter glass

---

[118] Ibid (42:58) and (43:08) respectively. See also Dogman Encounters Radio interviews, Parts 1 and 2 (Episode 233) and the Bonus Episode (Episode 234), described above.
[119] Ibid.

HEAD	Dog-like
FUR	Like a chow, but no strange smell to it
SNOUT	Lips more retractable than a humans, very sharp teeth
EARS	Pointed with tufts of hair
EYES	Amber colored like an illuminated glass of beer
ARMS	Exactly like the werewolf in *Van Helsing*
HANDS	Wolf's paw "blown up," five elongated fingers, rough, chapped skin - like the pad a dog has on his paws, long, thick fingernails/claws of about an inch or so
TORSO	Exactly like the werewolf in *Van Helsing*
LEGS	Exactly like the werewolf in *Van Helsing*
TAIL	Yes

What I find fascinating is how this topic of Dogman and the notion of people disappearing without a trace connects to the research of David Paulides: *Missing 411.* Is this creature responsible, at least in part, for some of these wholly strange disappearances? NM brings this topic up during his interview with Vic Cundiff.[120] Paulides, as far as I can tell, does NOT believe this to be the case. However, a keen investigator, he does not make reckless suppositions. Paulides will tell you that he only makes conclusions based upon fact.

There are many alleged Dogman images available online. Recently, I came across alleged Dogman footage.[121] This is by far the best digital footage I've seen of a

---

[120] Dogman Encounters Radio, "My Uncles Killed a Dogman! (Dogman Encounters Episode 66)," YouTube, October 21, 2015 (40:15-41:25). Retrieved 11/15/2020: https://www.youtube.com/watch?v=OXi6Umu6pWg.

[121] The Dalton Edwards Effect, "Dalton and Zach React to Groundbreaking "Dogman" Footage," YouTube, November 24, 2020 (6:07-6:11). Retrieved 12/19/2020: https://www.youtube.com/watch?v=8LLIUDI53KA&feature=youtu.be.

prospective Dogman creature. Yes, it could be fake. Yet, I don't know enough about how the process could be done to be able to dismiss this as fake.

Further, given the context of how the Facebook personality created the footage via a live event, this adds credibility to this Dogman footage. Admittedly, there is not a clear view, but it is enough to see that the subject is something massive. I suppose it could be a person, or someone in a suit, but the subject - an alleged Dogman - looks too real, albeit with a tinge of surreality.[122] It's as if my eyes see it, but my mind is saying, "This cannot be." THAT doubt makes the

---

[122] I spoke to my daughter on Saturday, December 19, 2020, around 1:15 PM. I asked her to look at the above referenced Dalton Footage of the alleged Dogman running across the yard. She told me something interesting about the Dogman creature: "It's not a living creature you can touch. It's paranormal." My daughter went on to state that she believes Dogman is an evil entity if you will. I find this notion of the creature being an evil entity a distinct possibility, which corresponds with my belief that this particular footage appears "with a tinge of surreality," but it does not jive with the many people who have had close contact with this creature, including Victor, who states that the Dogman is a living, breathing creature.

footage naturally appear awkward and phony.

Interestingly, I notice that the physical makeup of the subject appears to be almost lopsided with a large upper body and skinny lower body, almost like an inverted triangle with the base at top and the tip at the bottom. This is a common eyewitness characterization of the Dogman: massive like a bodybuilder with strong, muscular legs - yet skinnier and out of proportion with the upper body.

Note: The best photo I've ever seen has to be the alleged California Redwoods picture of a "Dogman" nonchalantly walking through the woods apparently with people nearby running away in horror.[123] It's also described as having been taken in North Carolina, but originally this photo was labeled as taken in the Redwoods of California, and so I tend to believe that's the true origin of this image.

---

[123] Reinier, Michael, "Dogman Photos from Northern California," Pinterest.com, June 2020. Retrieved 12/19/2020: https://www.pinterest.com/pin/151292868718286617/.

Perhaps of note is that I originally thought that this creature must be a Werewolf based on looks alone (it reminds me of Lon Chaney, Jr's depiction thereof in the famed horror film, *The Wolfman*, 1941[124]), but now realize it cannot be so. For, with what I know now based upon the eyewitness description of Victor, the US Government agent who works with what I've dubbed their "Men in Black" for cryptids, *this is a Dogman* and not a Werewolf based upon the tall and pointy ears alone.[125]

My point in mentioning this is that many times, I note that some witnesses will automatically describe their encounters as being one where they cross paths with a "werewolf" not understanding the distinctions between the two cryptids. I think this is simply proof that the Dogman, in our mind and psyche, is a rather recent phenomenon and that most people are

---

[124] Wikipedia: The Wolf Man (1941 Film).

[125] Dogman Encounters with Jeffrey Nadolny, passim. Again, by Nadolny's own accounting, there are at least fifty engrossing videos of Victor. This man could teach a class at a major university - he is that interesting to listen to.

either unaware or unfamiliar with the distinct characteristics between said creatures.

CH V: JOSH TURNER ACCOUNTS

I grappled with the idea of what to do with the following information obtained from one of the most interesting eyewitnesses and researchers I've ever encountered in any topic - hands down: Josh Turner of Central Texas. His information is so voluminous and unique that I determined that Turner warrants his own chapter. His nickname just happens to be "Wolf."

Whereas some eyewitness accounts tend to focus upon what the Dogman looks like, others focus on how the Dogman behaved. This brings me to perhaps the most comprehensive collection of Dogman accounts (albeit most are secondary): Texan Josh Turner. He is featured in several *Dogman Encounters Radio* episodes (55,

58, 59, 116[126]) which are almost entirely "edge of your seat," and "Holy crap - that cannot be!" in caliber.

It's interesting, and perhaps fits Turner's personality, although he admits that he tends to focus on details thanks to the advice of an ex-girlfriend of his, for his accounts tend to describe the behaviors as opposed to what they looked like. Which is perfectly fine. Frankly, I learned a lot about how these creatures tend to behave by listening over and over to Turner's accounts.

I also found it really interesting that Turner clearly states that he has no interest in hunting the Dogman or even seeing it

---

[126] Dogman Encounters Radio, "Dogman Encounters Episode 55," YouTube, August 12, 2015. Retrieved 11/21/2020: https://www.youtube.com/watch?v=YqUNaPtXLqk; Dogman Encounters Radio, "Dogman Encounters Episode 58," YouTube, September 2, 2015. Retrieved 11/21/2020: https://www.youtube.com/watch?v=A26IZtwyTBg; Dogman Encounters Radio, "Dogman Encounters Episode 59," YouTube, September 9, 2015. Retrieved 11/21/2020: https://www.youtube.com/watch?v=4wSKt0AtY1g; Dogman Encounters Radio, "Dogman Encounters Episode 116," YouTube, October 7, 2016. Retrieved 11/21/2020: https://www.youtube.com/watch?v=MF-3iK0YJZI.

again. He's seen plenty.[127] Yet, I'm writing this book in part as preparation for creating a team to go out and search for Dogman's presence. Maybe I'm just crazy.

Mind you, I wholeheartedly respect and honor the creature's prowess and power and place in nature, but I just have it burned in my soul that I want to at least see one from a distance - if that's even possible. Frankly, I have no pretensions about how dangerous these creatures are.

Again, every single source I cite here in *My Search for Dogman* primer is a "Crème de la Crème" of sorts of all of the sources out there. Therefore, I highly recommend and fervently hope that you seek these out, enjoy them, ponder their meanings, and *share them with others*. After all, what good is a good story if it's not shared with other good people? Again, if

---

[127] Dogman Encounters Radio, "Dogman Encounters Episode 116," YouTube, October 7, 2016. Retrieved 11/21/2020: https://www.youtube.com/watch?v=MF-3iK0YJZI (1:23:00-1:23:23). In fact, Josh Turner states, "I think that these people . . . [are] crazy."

you're able, please support these great sources anyway you can.

Back to Josh Turner's wealth of knowledge about Dogman. I consider him a modern day Brothers Grimm[128] for Dogman with his vast collection of Texas Dogman stories - and state this unequivocally with respect. I've listed some of his findings here based upon which *Dogman Encounters Radio* (DER) episode in which it is found, although there are other sources Turner has been cited in, too. Where possible, I include a specific citation to pinpoint the information for you, the reader.

In his accounts, Turner shares several truly frightening stories which were recounted to him by eyewitnesses directly or indirectly. He stresses several times that the listener can believe him or not. Turner does not care. He is only repeating what he was told and is not verifying the veracity of the accounts, though he has no doubt the

---

[128] Wikipedia: Brothers Grimm.

eyewitnesses are speaking what they believe to be true.

JOSH TURNER DER 55 - This episode mainly covers Turner's childhood growing up in Taylor, Texas, some 34 miles northeast of Austin. Point of fact, I have found in my research that Texas seems to have the most Dogman accounts, followed by Tennessee, Ohio, and Michigan. He recounts how he was chased by a Dogman all the way home when he was about twelve years old.

The experience scared the heck out of Turner (as it would all of us), but made him realize - through his quest to understand what he saw - that many, many people like himself saw something similar; and it's OK. It is what it is. Dogman exists and life goes on. These stories, according to Turner, all involve the State of Texas. Again, they are simplified and condensed, so please, nothing will sound better than these rhetorical sounds bouncing directly from Turner's realistic lips to your eager ears....

JOSH TURNER DER 58 - One story involves a kid who was playing with some friends in a tree fort near a cemetery, they heard strange noises in the tree line, were spooked, and left. The kids believed they were followed by something which paralleled their path. That night, the eyewitness told Turner that he heard a noise at his window, opened the blind, and saw a Dogman licking the glass of his bedroom window.[129]

Another story involves some kids who drove to an old, abandoned German church and were inside rummaging around, exploring, when one of the younger eyewitnesses told Turner that he looked out of the back window of this church and spotted several Dogmen climbing out from an abandoned well: first one, then another, then another, and another.

Finally, he got the attention of the ambivalent elder teen girl (who had found a

____

[129] Dogman Encounters Radio, "Dogman Encounters Episode 58," YouTube, September 2, 2015 (10:12-13:42). Retrieved 11/21/2020: https://www.youtube.com/watch?v=A26lZtwyTBg.

crucifix in a nearby room and pocketed it as a souvenir) and her teen boyfriend, and they all panicked, scattered, and hid in the main sanctuary of this old church.

Low and behold, a Dogman tried to enter the church, all the while the elderly teen girl and boy, clutching this crucifix tightly, prayed intently to themselves. The Dogman inexplicably left. (The teen girl later said that it appeared the Dogman was afraid of the church - a sanctuary of sorts, of the crucifix, of her prayer, of God Almighty.) The group finally escaped to their car out front which, interestingly enough, had an open back door, and the smell of urine on the back seat. The eyewitness believed that God had saved them from the evil Dogman.[130]

A third story involved a hunter who was out "in the bush" trying to kill a wild hog. In a blind in a tree, this hunter heard what appeared to be a Dogman climbing his tree. Not sure what to do, and panicking, he

---

[130] Ibid (23:54-31:10).

grabbed a dog whistle he had in his pocket, blew it, and "the noise stopped."

What's really interesting to me was that the Dogman walked away and to the hunter's astonishment, the Dogman threw his hands up (Note - hands, and not paws!) as if to say, "What's up?" My interpretation of the Dogman's gesture, which is based upon the totality of the event, was more of a "Piss off!" or "F*ck off!" gesture. The hunter said that, after realizing the intelligence of this creature, he shouted, "What's your name?" Dogman simply barked and continued to walk off with two other creatures.[131]

JOSH TURNER DER 59 - In this episode, Turner explains how he has begun to research the Dogman - not just as a local phenomenon, but also for examples of the same throughout the world and throughout history. Truthfully, I was stunned by some

---

[131] Ibid (57:50-1:03:31).

of Turner's research claims.[132] He describes verifiable facts and legends such as…

1) The Ancient Egyptians had of course Anubis, the Egyptian God of the Dead;

2) The Greeks had extensive literary and cultural references to the word "cynocephaly," which is Latin but originates from the Greek (as does a lot of Latin language and culture) and means "dog" (cyno) and "head" (cephaly);

3) Turner incredulously states that King Darius III of Persia (basically what is now Egypt, Turkey, Iraq, Iran, and all the way to Western India[133]) used Dogmen soldiers against the Greek Army led by Alexander the Great - apparently in the

---

[132] Dogman Encounters Radio, "Dogman Encounters Episode 59," YouTube, September 9, 2015. Retrieved 11/21/2020: https://www.youtube.com/watch?v=4wSKt0AtY1g. See also Wikipedia: Cynocephaly.

[133] Ancient Civilizations, "Persian Empire," AncientEmpiresBlog.wordpress.com, Date Unknown. Retrieved 11/22/2020: https://ancientempiresblog.wordpress.com/persian/.

Battle of Issus (333 BC) and/or Gaugamela (331 BC).[134]

These soldiers apparently came from what is now Turkey (Anatolian peninsula) and were used *as mercenaries*.[135] Turner notes in his research that these dogmen reportedly spoke a sort of barking language and some subsets of this group even wore standard clothing to "fit in" with the surrounding civilizations[136];

4) Even the great Portuguese explorer, Ferdinand Magellan, flying under the flag of Spain (1520), claimed to have encountered these creatures (Or, frankly, are they really a race of people?) in Patagonia in South America (southernmost portion of the continent) where "they saw these dog-headed men with these giant feet."[137]

---

[134] Wikipedia: Battle of Issus and Battle of Gaugamela.

[135] Dogman Encounters Radio, "Dogman Encounters Episode 59," YouTube, September 9, 2015 (23:15-23:53). Retrieved 11/22/2020: https://www.youtube.com/watch?v=4wSKt0AtY1g.

[136] Ibid (26:05-26:52).

[137] Ibid (25:47-25:55).

5) St. Christopher (Patron Saint of Travelers), of the Eastern Orthodox Church (which essentially split off from the Roman Catholic Church in 1054 during what was known as the Great Schism[138], although this break took many years to evolve) was believed to have been a Dogman based upon some reports, according to Turner. He adds that these same reports indicate St. Christopher's appearance changed to human form as a result of his love for God and becoming a Christian.[139]

In fact, there are controversial dog-headed religious icons of St. Christopher . . . *with a dog's head.* And, this seemingly unusual religious iconography is not limited to St. Christopher. It's actually quite stunning and intriguing.[140]

---

[138] Wikipedia: East-West Schism.

[139] Dogman Encounters Radio, "Dogman Encounters Episode 59," YouTube, September 9, 2015 (28:50-29:20). Retrieved 11/22/2020: https://www.youtube.com/watch?v=4wSKt0AtY1g.

[140] Pageau, Jonathan, "Understanding the Dog-Headed Icon of St. Christopher" (Post 1 of 2), OrthodoxArtsJournal.org, July 8, 2013. Retrieved 11/22/2020: https://orthodoxartsjournal.org/the-icon-of-st-christopher/.

Yet, Catholic scholar Jonathan Pageau argues - quite cogently - that the icons are mere religious representations and not true depictions of St. Christopher. He states: "What appears at the edge of Man is analogous to what appears at the edge of the world both in spatial and temporal terms, so the barbarians, dog-headed men or other monsters on the spatial boundaries of civilization and the temporal end of civilization are akin to the death and animality which is the corporal spatial limit of an individual and the final temporal end of earthly life."[141] In other words, these religious icons depicting Dogmen are meant to be symbolic, metaphorical - not literal.

Interestingly, Pageau also notes that "in our savvy scientific age, no one believes

---

Pageau, Jonathan, "Understanding the Dog-Headed Icon of St. Christopher" (Post 2 of 2), OrthodoxArtsJournal.org, August 26, 2013. Retrieved 11/22/2020: https://orthodoxartsjournal.org/the-dog-headed-icon-of-st-christopher-pt-2-encountering-saint-christopher/. This is a lengthy, well-documented study worth inclusion here.

[141] Ibid (Part 1 of 2, Paragraph 7).

in dog-headed men and races of giants anymore."[142] To this I add, "Oh, really?"

Prior to sainthood, St. Christopher was martyred circa 251 AD by beheading at the hands of a local king in the ancient City of Lycia. His crime? Trying to turn people into followers of Christ.

6) In Anatolia, in what is now Eastern Turkey, Turner states that the aforementioned reports indicate there existed to the effect the "City of the Dogmen." This would make some sense if King Darius III of Persia used Dogmen as mercenaries against Alexander the Great for Anatolia was part and parcel of King Darius' northern empire.[143] If true, it also adds credence to the story of St. Christopher being a Dogman.

JOSH TURNER DER 116 - This is perhaps Turner's best episode. By now, you can hear he's polished his craft of

---

[142] Ibid (Part 1 of 2, Second-to-last paragraph).
[143] Dogman Encounters Radio, "Dogman Encounters Episode 59," YouTube, September 9, 2015, (29:25-29:32). Retrieved 11/22/2020: https://www.youtube.com/watch?v=4wSKt0AtY1g.

storytelling, and has really gone "full throttle" in researching the topic of Dogman and interviewing a multitude of eyewitnesses to Dogman.

One of the most chilling eyewitness accounts I've ever heard (granted this story was told to Turner by the eyewitness who in turn shares it with us) is that of "Robbie" - not his real name.[144] I think Robbie learned a most valuable lesson: You should not bicker with your mom when you know she has nothing but your best interest at heart . . . and she wants you to come home early.

Robbie was in a tree stand hunting wild hogs, in spite of his mom's plea for him to come home. He saw what he thought was a large creature hidden in the brush some 75 yards distant, but he wasn't sure what it was. Robbie wanted to shoot it and whistled at it. At that point, the Dogman started walking toward him. It walked like a man, and swung its arms like a man would.

---

[144] Ibid (27:55-46:55).

Robbie broke into prayer and suddenly heard a hog and her piglets. He felt this was a God-send. The Dogman started to focus on these hogs. But was "sniffing the air" when Robbie tried to egress from the tree stand and the door squeaked. He made a break for his ATV . . . and the Dogman chased him.

Robbie finally reached a pasture which contained an extremely mean Braford bull and a lot of potholes. Driving his ATV as carefully as he could, all the while tempering the speed with the pot holes, Robbie had the bull chasing him from the direction of 9 O'clock, and the Dogman from the direction of 6 O'clock, as he headed for the tree at 12 O'clock.

Robbie climbed up this "tree of life" and awaited his fate, the Dogman laying flat on the pasture a short distance away, and the bull under the tree. Luckily, his *loving mother* sent his brothers to look for him. When the brothers arrived, they were shocked as to why Robbie was hiding in the tree. They did not notice the Dogman initially, but did see it. All were stunned by the creature when it stood up and sauntered off into the dark woodline. Again, as with all of the other sources I cite herein, it would behoove the reader to listen to this source front to back, perhaps more than once or twice. Josh Turner's stories are absolutely incredible...

Josh "Wolf" Turner Addict? Additional Known Sources
Dogman Encounters Radio, "Dogman Encounters Episode 136," YouTube, February 24, 2017. Retrieved 11/22/2020: https://www.youtube.com/watch?v=cWcRqpqXJEg (46:58).
Dogman Encounters Radio, "Dogman Encounters Episode 137," YouTube, March 3, 2017. Retrieved 11/22/2020: https://www.youtube.com/watch?v=USX3mss2f9k (1:08:48).
Dogman Encounters Radio, "Dogman Encounters Episode 162," YouTube, August 25, 2017. Retrieved 11/22/2020: https://www.youtube.com/watch?v=Zek7JdNDzCo (2:30:32).
Dogman Encounters Radio, "Dogman Encounters Episode 169," YouTube, October 13, 2017. Retrieved 11/22/2020: https://www.youtube.com/watch?v=eqCVXZlXQN8 (1:13:55).
Paranormal Round Table, "EP40 - Hyena Cryptids," YouTube, October 4, 2019.

Retrieved 11/22/2020: https://www.youtube.com/watch?v=DtXWXdxIkPE (1:04:24).

The Venomous Fringe, "Dogman Phenomenon - Interview with Josh Turner," YouTube, April 23, 2019. Retrieved 11/22/2020: https://www.youtube.com/watch?v=rGmYBgtsBYo (2:51:06).

CH VI: ORIGINS - DOGMAN AND WEREWOLF

What are these creatures, really? Where do they come from? I have so many questions but not enough answers. Are they: Natural? Spiritual? Interstellar? A military experiment?

The late famed psychic and spiritual teacher Sylvia Browne has interesting assumptions about cryptids, two in particular: Bigfoot and Werewolf. Regarding the former, although Browne tends to take a spiritual view of most things, she seems to think that Bigfoot could be a real creature. Browne even addresses the fact that so many cultures throughout the world recognize Bigfoot in some form and label.[145]

My wife and I are students of Sylvia Browne's spiritual teachings. Some of you may already remember she was a frequent

---

[145] Browne, Sylvia, *Secrets & Mysteries of the World*, Hay House, Inc., 2005, 54-57.

guest on the *Montel Williams Show* back in the 1990s. We went to one of her lectures around 2009 in San Bernardino and we got to meet her. My wife actually shook Sylvia Browne's hand. It was a powerful moment for my wife and me.

Though my wife, psychic and author Debbie Dombrow Hoffmann, has read just about every book ever written by Sylvia Browne (25-30 books), I must admit I have read perhaps 4-5 of them. However, if interested in Sylvia Brown and/or psychic phenomenon, I highly recommend that you read Browne's great memoir, *Adventures of a Psychic*.[146] That's an exciting read!

Regarding the Werewolf, Browne does not see them as actual creatures, rather as the result of a medical-emotional state: "I'm convinced that the werewolf phenomenon originated from diseases such as porphyria, the intake of ergot-infested grain in the diet,

---

[146] Browne, Sylvia, May, Antoinette, *Adventures of a Psychic: The Fascinating and Inspiring True-Life Story of One of America's Most Successful Clairvoyants,* Hay House, Inc., 1998.

and the medicinal remedies that were used at the time."[147] Naturally, though I have yet to see one, I believe the evidence is too overwhelming, and that at least some of them are actual, living, breathing creatures.

I was listening to an interesting podcast this morning (12/8/2020): Paranormal Portal. The host, Brent Thomas, and a sidekick (Don Longbeard), were discussing the issue of Dogman, which lately has been par for the course for my research - but then they breached a topic which caught my attention: is Dogman a spiritual being of sorts that can travel between different dimensions.

The evidence referenced emanates from the famous Skinwalker Ranch near Ballard, Utah. Longbeard states that during an investigation at this ranch, and using infrared (IR) cameras, investigators "saw a portal open and out came a dogman."[148]

---

[147] Browne, Sylvia, *Secrets & Mysteries of the World*, Hay House, Inc., 2005, 80-81.
[148] Paranormal Portal [Brent Thomas], "21 - The Dogman Phenomena," Revolver Podcasts, June 14, 2019 (16:30-17:00).

Later in the episode, Thomas discusses who I've dubbed the "Dogmother of the Dogman phenomena," Linda Godfrey. She was on his podcast previously[149] and discussed similar issues related to this notion that Dogman is somehow connected to portals. He notes how Godfrey used trail cams operating at three frames per second to record stationary and secured deer carcasses that clearly appear in one frame and then literally disappear within a few foggy frames of footage.[150]

Victor told *Dogman Encounters with Jeffrey Nadolny* that Werewolves (not to be confused with Dogmen) are trained like Marines with a 12 week "boot camp" of sorts. Victor states that these creatures are

---

[149] See Paranormal Portal Episode "37 - Linda Godfrey on Bigfoot Part 1" (July 19, 2019) and Episode "40 - Linda Godfrey on Bigfoot Part 2" (July 26, 2019).

[150] Ibid (17:00-17:47). To go one step further, check out investigative journalist Paul Beben's *Paranormal Declassified*, "Chasing Skinwalkers," December 28, 2020 (S1 E2). In this fascinating episode on Travel Channel, Bebel interviews a man who owns a farm along Bray Road near Elkhorn, Wisconsin. The man shows palpable proof that these creatures possibly generate and/or move through mist-like portals. Strange!

as smart as any average human, much faster, and much stronger. He claims that Werewolves are typically used in Black Ops to extract individuals from captivity.[151]

Hence, Victor states that the Werewolf is a "military asset."[152] They are essentially "super soldiers" who are trained in a program in Virginia to help fight for the US Government. Along the lines of the Werewolf being a "super soldier," another eyewitness on Nadolny's podcast affirms this notion.

Guest John B states that the Werewolf is not only a super soldier, but that the concept thereof "started with Hitler and the

---

[151] Dogman Encounters with Jeffrey Nadolny, "Dogman Subscriber Call-Ins Q&A with Gov't Agent Victor]," YouTube, November 22, 2020 (30:26-32:30). Retrieved 11/28/2020: https://www.youtube.com/watch?v=_3GOpXVprdE.
[152] Dogman Encounters with Jeffrey Nadolny, "Dogman Subscriber Call-Ins Q&A with Gov't Agent Round 2," YouTube, November 25, 2020 (20:31-22:52). Retrieved 11/28/2020: https://www.youtube.com/watch?v=MnQhPCYsmSl.

Nazis."[153] What's really interesting to me, almost unbelievable, is that these creatures sometimes "go rogue" - for whatever reason - and Victor and his team have to hunt them down.

However, Victor states that the Werewolves are always given a choice: go back into the program in Virginia or die. (Remember, Victor states that Werewolves speak English.) Sadly, most choose death. They apparently just do not want to live that controlled life anymore. It almost sounds to me like a regular human soldier's PTSD - crazy, huh? A Werewolf with PTSD. If the creature does go back, it is retrained, rehabilitated, relocated to a new habitat, and then monitored very closely.[154]

In a chilling soliloquy, Victor reveals that due to an Executive Order, the US Government releases creatures regularly.

---

[153] Dogman Encounters with Jeffrey Nadolny, "Dogman Former Military and Policeman John B. Discusses Dogman and DogmanCams.com," YouTube, October 26, 2020, (32:53-33:19). Retrieved 12/28/2020: https://www.youtube.com/watch?v=J6uyaVSSjwY.
[154] Ibid.

I'm assuming he means a combination of Dogman and Werewolf, but Victor seems to indicate government involvement in Bigfoot, too.[155]

Along this line of thinking, a cursory analysis of a general map depicting major US military installations is quite interesting.[156] Many of the states indicated on the map fully correspond with being what I would call "hot spots" of Dogman activity, if not Werewolf and Bigfoot as well. With the exception of Alaska, Colorado, Georgia, and Florida, I consider the remaining states as truly active Dogman areas of the country.

Given this information, my theory that there is a correlation between sightings of these creatures (Victor calls the Dogman,

---

[155] Dogman Encounters with Jeffrey Nadolny, "Dogman Subscriber Call-Ins Q&A with Gov't Agent Victor]," YouTube, November 22, 2020 (55:33-55:40). Retrieved 11/28/2020: https://www.youtube.com/watch?v=_3GOpXVprdE.

[156] Smith. Stewart, "Major U.S. MIlitary Bases and Installations," TheBalanceCareers.com, November 20, 2019. Retrieved 12/29/2020: https://www.thebalancecareers.com/us-military-major-bases-4061575.

Werewolf, and Bigfoot the "Big Three") and military installations (i.e. they are "released" at these points) seems cogent and reasonable.

CH VII: DOGMAN CHARACTERISTICS

This chapter was actually one of the first I penciled in for this book and one of the funnest chapters which was created. I really enjoyed the process. In effect, it's the end result of all of my many hours spent listening to podcasts, taking notes, pondering, and documenting; the synthesis of everything I've learned so far about Dogman - and in an unexpected, ancillary way, the Werewolf.

These General Characteristics of the Dogman are based upon a myriad of testimonies from dozens of witnesses and are designed to show you, the reader, what you can expect from a Dogman *if you happen to have the fortune (or misfortune)* of encountering one of these creatures.

Thus, given the confusion which could arise when an eyewitness sees a Dogman and erroneously notes it's a Werewolf, or vice versa, it is possible that some of these characteristics cited from a specific source could be in error. However, I do feel confident that the following overview is quite accurate. Also, where possible, the source from whence the information came is cited.

HABITAT - Quite interesting is that most eyewitness accounts about Dogman involve forest and woods, but there are some which actually involve urban areas.[157] The eyewitness named Victor (a US Government agent now retired), interviewed over fifty times by *Dogman Encounters with Jeffrey Nadolny,* discusses the issue of city versus urban habitation of the dogman. It's interesting to hear his response: "I've been

---

[157] Anonymous, "San Mateo County, CA Encounter," DogmanEncounters.com, August 27, 2016. Retrieved 11/11/2020: https://dogmanencounters.com/san-mateo-county-ca-encounter/; See also Dogman Encounters Radio, "Dogman Encounters Episode 115," YouTube, September 30, 2016. Retrieved 12/29/2020: https://www.youtube.com/watch?v=4N3YIX3C7x0,

to just about every big city in the nation - and removed 'em."[158]

In a recent episode of *Dogman Encounters with Jeffrie Nadolny,* Victor was sent to a pizzeria in Atlanta, Georgia, to remove a nuisance creature.[159] It turned out to be a Werewolf. He found the creature hiding out in the basement, and he struck up a conversation with said creature, which he claims is quite normal with Werewolves: "There's one way out of this . . . You can live or you can die . . . You can walk out of here and get into the back of this black vehicle, we'll go back to Virginia [to the breeding center], or I'll kill you right here or you can kill me."[160] Incidentally, according to Victor,

---

[158] Dogman Encounters with Jeffrey Nadolny, "Dogman Subscriber Call-Ins Q&A with Gov't Agent Victor]," YouTube, November 22, 2020 (28:32-28:50). Retrieved 11/28/2020: https://www.youtube.com/watch?v=_3GOpXVprdE.

[159] Dogman Encounters with Jeffrey Nadolny, "Dogman Gov't Agent Victor Shares the St. Louis Hunt," YouTube, December 10, 2020. Retrieved 12/11/2020: https://www.youtube.com/watch?v=83IISiJeTx4.

[160] Ibid (29:17-29:42). Interestingly, Victor apparently inadvertently admits that his name is Col. Johnson. I can therefore assume through previous interviews that it is Col. William "Bill" Johnson of the alleged US Government Breeding Program. I could be wrong.

this is only one of two werewolves which ever agreed to go back. The rest chose death - for whatever reason.

STRANGE SILENCE - More times than not, eyewitnesses describe a "Strange silence" when Dogman comes around. The normal animal activity in the wild literally ceases to make noise (birds, crickets, etc.). In a *Dogman Encounters Radio* episode[161], "Brad" (who resides in Northeast Riverside County, California) adds to the chilling characteristic of a strange silence that whenever he goes hiking, he feels like he is being watched.

The following eyewitness account has a serious organic ambience to it. It's no doubt real, first hand knowledge of someone who's seen the Dogman up close and personal. The entire account is quite chilling, and again, I suggest you read it in its entirety, but the following excerpt struck

---

[161] Dogman Encounters Radio, "Dogman Encounters Episode 268 (Boss Dogman!)," YouTube, September 6, 2019 (17:28-17:31). Retrieved 12/29/2020: https://www.youtube.com/watch?v=djbSdp1LB-U.

me as extremely pertinent to this characteristic and nicely embroiders this base fear...

"Not too long ago, in the late '90's, my uncle and my dad, who had come down from Missouri to visit, decided to venture into those same woods [where a Dogman was spotted] in front of my aunt's house. They took a couple of pistols and two rifles and were gone for several hours . . . They both experienced the feeling of being watched and felt an uneasiness that 'something' just wasn't right. The area where the sawmill was had no life stirring around it. No birds, no squirrels, no crickets, no bugs, even the small pond was still and lifeless. They couldn't shake the feeling of being observed by a secret watcher and both swore they saw a large

> black shadow lurking in the shade of one of the mysteriously dug caves."[162]

DIABOLICAL - Dogman is definitely an intelligent creature, cunning, shrewd - diabolical, and will toy with your fears and emotions.[163] Dogman has been known to even grin at their unexpected victims.[164] Furthermore, many people *feel* evil emanating from these creatures, like Tim Coonbo Baker: "The thing that got me [was] . . . the evil that they [eyewitnesses] felt from that thing [Dogman or Werewolf]."[165]

---

[162] J Thompson1, "The Beast of LBL (Land between the Lakes, Kentucky)," Reddit.com, 2013. Retrieved 11/24/2020: https://www.reddit.com/r/Thetruthishere/comments/18fog0/the_beast_of_lbl_land_between_the_lakes_kentucky/.

[163] Cryptids Canada, "Episode 123 Dogmen!!!! Will Eat You," YouTube, November 12, 2020 (9:43-9:49). Retrieved 12/29/2020: https://www.youtube.com/watch?v=0AsllGsU5Xo.

[164] Dogman Encounters Radio, "Dogman Encounters Episode 268 (Boss Dogman!)," YouTube, September 6, 2019 (28:27-28:34). Retrieved 12/29/2020: https://www.youtube.com/watch?v=djbSdp1LB-U.

[165] Dogman Encounters with Jeffrey Nadolny, "Dogman and Bigfoot Tim Coonbo Baker Discusses Both and Shares Encounters," YouTube, November 3, 2020 (51:09-51:16). Retrieved 12/18/2020: https://www.youtube.com/watch?v=vAnTs2qFV_M. Like

Typically, the Dogman will hide behind or even up in the trees. It has been known to slash tires with their sharp nails or flatten tires with thrown objects[166] . . . even follow people home.[167]

When prey is around (including humans), the creature will sniff the air to determine who or what is in the area.[168] Dogman will growl if threatened. It has been said to avoid looking at the creature in the eyes to not only avoid antagonizing it to attack, but also prevent nightmares.

According to Victor, the Werewolf is extremely intelligent and is at par with an

---

Victor, Baker will make you spellbound when he speaks about his many encounters. He, too, is a very credible witness.

[166] Dogman Encounters Radio, "Dogman Encounters Episode 51," YouTube, July 15, 2015 (36:25-39:17). Retrieved 11/26/2020: https://www.youtube.com/watch?v=dt0EI0oQ8Ok.

[167] Dogman Encounters Radio, "Dogman Encounters Episode 130," YouTube, January 13, 2017. Retrieved 12/29/2020: https://www.youtube.com/watch?v=TDQqIaIE3HI.

[168] Cryptids Canada, "Episode 123 Dogmen!!!! Will Eat You," YouTube, November 12, 2020 (9:43-9:49). Retrieved 12/29/2020: https://www.youtube.com/watch?v=0AsIIGsU5Xo; See also Dogman Encounters Radio, "Dogman Encounters Episode 116," YouTube, October 7, 2016. Retrieved 12/29/2020: https://www.youtube.com/watch?v=MF-3iK0YJZI&t=2835s.

average human. He states that on a hypothetical intelligence scale, a Werewolf is a 10/10, Bigfoot a 6 or 7/10, and Dogman a 4/10 (on par with a Chimpanzee) - yet devious and more aggressive than any of the other two creatures.[169]

Most encounters are with a lone Dogman, although a huge problem unforeseen by the US Government breeding program and their decision to "seed" the creatures throughout the US has arisen: Dogman likes to travel in packs. Now, this may seem logical to you and me, but to the breeder program officials (Think: bureaucrats!) - it did not.[170] As a result, Victor and his cryptid team have had to go out to areas like Pennsylvania to try and ameliorate the problem created by Dogman packs with upwards of some 200 members.

---

[169] Dogman Encounters with Jeffrey Nadolny, "Dogman Subscriber Call-ins With Victor Gov't Agent Part 3," YouTube, November 27, 2020 (1:28:47-1:29:28). Retrieved 12/30/2020: https://www.youtube.com/watch?v=WA0y8Olkls4&t=1569s.

[170] Dogman Encounters with Jeffrey Nadolny, "Dogman Gov't Agent William Shares More EP 44," YouTube, May 23, 2020. Retrieved 12/30/2020: https://www.youtube.com/watch?v=DG9kBd7MRx8.

If Dogman attacks in packs (perhaps as high as 20-30[171]), then their strategy is to kill you, and they will typically use flanking tactics, drawing your attention to one, while the others creep up behind you or from the sides.[172]

Sometimes, Dogman has been known to make sounds like a crying baby or a woman in distress.[173] When out in the

---

[171] Mattsquatch Presents, "The Dogman Cometh," YouTube, November 10, 2020. Retrieved 11/10/2020: https://www.youtube.com/watch?v=TO8I3DOKmlo. Although I've studied many eyewitness accounts, and most depict a single or perhaps Dogman duo, Mattsquatch states unequivocally in several sources that fairly large packs are the norm. God Help anybody who runs into that situation!

[172] Dogman Encounters Radio, "Dogman Encounters Episode 334 (Do You Want to Come with Me and Hunt a Dogman?)," YouTube, November 27, 2020 (1:01:00-1:01:36). Retrieved 11/27/2020: https://www.youtube.com/watch?v=efToo-CCyF0.

[173] Dogman Encounters Radio, "Dogman Encounters Episode 233 (Part 1) (A 1,000 Pound Dogman!)," YouTube, January 4, 2019. Retrieved 11/11/2020: https://www.youtube.com/watch?v=AyPVMHdfl6E&t=7s. Dogman Encounters Radio, "Dogman Encounters Episode 233 (A 1,000 Pound Dogman! (Part 2)," YouTube, January 11, 2019. Retrieved 11/11/2020: https://www.youtube.com/watch?v=bmY0Y1AzStc. Dogman Encounters Radio, "Dogman Encounters Episode 234 (A 1,000 Pound Dogman! (Bonus Episode)," YouTube, January 13, 2019. Retrieved 11/11/2020: https://www.youtube.com/watch?v=-AbOXjJC-mo.

woods, upon hearing these cries . . . beware. It is absolutely not prudent to seek the source of these sounds out, for some people have been killed by them. Listening to Adam Davis describe how he found bloody clothing (presumably belonging to a Dogman victim) near Germantown, Pennsylvania, is absolutely chilling and absolutely real.[174]

It has been stated by several eyewitnesses and experts in the field, including Victor the US Government agent, that it is never wise to use firearms against the Dogman - unless it's a last resort. The creature is known to seek revenge for itself and others in the pack.[175]

---

[174] Dogman Encounters Radio, "Dogman Encounters Episode 51," YouTube, July 15, 2015 (Circa 44:00). Retrieved 11/26/2020: https://www.youtube.com/watch?v=dt0El0oQ8Ok. See also Dogman Encounters Radio, "Dogman Encounters Episode 90," YouTube, April 13, 2016. Retrieved 12/30/2020: https://www.youtube.com/watch?v=lRlbSqSRadg&t=1s.

[175] Dogman Encounters Radio, "Dogman Encounters Episode 334 (Do You Want to Come with Me and Hunt a Dogman?)," YouTube, November 27, 2020 (54:10-54:40). Retrieved 11/27/2020: https://www.youtube.com/watch?v=efToo-CCyF0; See also Dogman Encounters with Jeffrey Nadolny, "Dogman Taylor Mississippi Family T*rror and Q&A with Gov't Agent EP

BIGFOOT INTERACTION - There is evidence that Dogman often lives in areas along with Bigfoot.[176] There is also evidence that Dogman does not get along with Bigfoot and has been known to kill Bigfoot, but the inverse is also true. Yet, Dogman is generally more aggressive than Bigfoot.

On the other hand, though Bigfoot is considered more docile than the Dogman and Werewolf, and has even been faced with teams of hunters, generally foreigners from Australia and New Zealand, trying to kill them[177], Victor states that Bigfoot will not allow a Dogman to stay in his habitat and will "force them out."[178]

36," YouTube, May 5, 2020 (18:18-19:43). Retrieved 1/2/2021: https://www.youtube.com/watch?v=jZSHLABsDp8.

[176] Dogman Encounters Radio, "Dogman Encounters Episode 233 (Part 1) (A 1,000 Pound Dogman!)," YouTube, January 4, 2019. Retrieved 11/11/2020: https://www.youtube.com/watch?v=AyPVMHdfI6E&t=7s. You have to listen to all of the DER episodes cited throughout this work involving this man, John. His closeness and interactions with both animals is unmatched anywhere I've researched.

[177] Dogman Encounters with Jeffrey Nadolny, "Dogman Gov't Agent William Shares More EP 44," YouTube, May 23, 2020. Retrieved 12/31/2020: https://www.youtube.com/watch?v=DG9kBd7MRx8.

[178] Ibid (44:15-44:31).

AGILE - What stuns me about this creature is that it can be hit with a high-powered round and not be affected.[179] The creature has nimble fingers (often described as racoon-like[180]) and can open doors and windows. Dogman is fast on two *or* four legs, can chase you down at high speeds, and runs at an angle.[181]

Victor states that the average Dogman can travel about 3,000 miles within 17 days. The average speed is about 22 miles per hour.[182] They typically run when they are traveling with a purpose.

---

[179] Dogman Encounters Radio, "Dogman Encounters Episode 268 (Boss Dogman!)," YouTube, September 6, 2019 (41:31-42:07). Retrieved 12/29/2020: https://www.youtube.com/watch?v=djbSdp1LB-U.

[180] Dogman Encounters Radio, "Dogman Encounters Episode 51," YouTube, July 15, 2015. Retrieved 11/26/2020: https://www.youtube.com/watch?v=dt0EI0oQ8Ok.

[181] Dogman Encounters Radio, "Dogman Terrorizes Man While He Was Driving Down a Road! (Dogman Encounters Episode 117)," YouTube, October 14, 2016 (19:00-24:20). Retrieved 12/29/2020: https://www.youtube.com/watch?v=WTLpjAxgSz8.

[182] Dogman Encounters with Jeffrey Nadolny, "Dogman Subscriber Call-Ins Q&A with Gov't Agent Round 2," YouTube, November 25, 2020 (50:00-50:20). Retrieved 11/28/2020: https://www.youtube.com/watch?v=MnQhPCYsmSl.

Dogman has an incredible, natural ability, well documented, to avoid headshots.[183]

TRAVEL - It has been theorized that Dogman uses waterways as roads, for they use the water to cover their scent and avoid being tracked. In spite of seeing one which he describes as black and racoon-like, one eyewitness is grateful for the experience, stating it was "One of the coolest, most unique things I think I've ever experienced in my life."[184]

Though stealth is the way of the Dogman, with the physical characteristics sometimes described as a large wolf with a large head, some are nonchalant about their

---

[183] Dogman Encounters Radio, "Dogman Encounters Episode 334 (Do You Want to Come with Me and Hunt a Dogman?)," YouTube, November 27, 2020 (1:02:23-1:05:18). Retrieved 11/27/2020: https://www.youtube.com/watch?v=efToo-CCyF0.

[184] Dogman Encounters with Jeffrey Nadolny, "Officer Shares His Terrifying Encounter," YouTube, November 10, 2020 (6:30-8:02 and 13:26-13:29). Retrieved 11/14/2020: https://www.youtube.com/watch?v=_rmYgaHnSwc&feature=youtu.be.

presence, their surroundings, and being seen, particularly by humans.[185]

DEALING WITH DOGMAN - If you are lucky enough to have been able to avoid this creature in your life, more power to you. If, however, this is not the case, here are some tips to coping with the beast.

Though he stands clearly against the notion of hunting a Dogman, Larry Parker discusses the issue of utilizing a proper reconnaissance methodology if that were the case (49:48-50:44).[186] Like Sun Tzu, Parker states that you have to know your enemy beforehand.[187] Know how the creature behaves. What are its habits? How does it move in the forest?

Parker duly notes that hunting an aggressive Dogman in many respects is a lot

---

[185] Dogman Encounters Radio, "Dogman Encounters Episode 332 (Frank Sobczak's Dogman Encounter)," YouTube, November 13, 2020 (38:00-47:00). Retrieved 11/14/2020: https://www.youtube.com/watch?v=N2_5BFO3Q0g.

[186] Dogman Encounters Radio, "I Shot a Dogman with a .30-06 Rifle! (Dogman Encounters Episode 21)," YouTube, February 17, 2015, (circa 8:02). Retrieved 11/9/2020: https://www.youtube.com/watch?v=YlVn-GJJxYk.

[187] Wikipedia: The Art of War.

like hunting an aggressive human - as in combat. Whereas the human is trying to kill you, you must assume the Dogman is likewise trying to kill you. It's that simple.

Besides Larry Parker's interaction in Northern Michigan, I've only heard of two other accounts where an eyewitness shot at a Dogman and both accounts took place in Oklahoma, another Dogman hotspot.[188]

By most accounts, Dogman is extremely intelligent, shrewd, and cunning. Parker recommends setting up several game cameras *prior to* "the hunt." This photographic evidence will help you to answer some of the aforementioned questions.

One eyewitness even states that wearing a strong perfume in the wild is not

---

[188] Dogman Encounters Radio, "Dogman Encounters Episode 334 (Do You Want to Come with Me and Hunt a Dogman?)," YouTube, November 27, 2020. Retrieved 11/27/2020: https://www.youtube.com/watch?v=efToo-CCyF0. The eyewitness claims that the Dogman had "two .416 Rigbys in him" (52:35-52:50). For what it's worth, and I don't mean to sound pious, but I find the circumstances of the wounding of this Dogman repulsive.

prudent.[189] The smell can at the minimum alert the creature - be it the Dogman, Werewolf, or perhaps Bigfoot - that you're there in their habitat, or even incite the creature to violence.

Without a doubt, the *expert in the field* of Dogman is Victor. He has some expert suggestions for dealing with this creature which everyone should heed. These are some of his main points...

Lighting is a good deterrent (12 feet or higher); a concealed nail board is also a good deterrent;[190]

When confronted by a Dogman, repeatedly "look down and glance up," always noting the Dogman's movement, but

[189] Bigfoot Crossroads, "The Dogman of LBL Bigfoot Outlaw Radio EP 40 Part 3," YouTube, November 2, 2017 (00:35-1:00). Retrieved 12/10/2020: https://www.youtube.com/watch?v=DnRxX-qCUtY.

[190] Dogman Encounters with Jeffrey Nadolny, "Dogman Subscriber Call-Ins with Victor Gov't Agent Part 3," YouTube, November 27, 2020. Retrieved 11/28/2020: https://www.youtube.com/watch?v=WA0y8OIkls4.

never look directly into the creature's eyes or stare;[191]

The best defense is to avoid Dogman at all costs. Firearms will help, but avoid use of them at all costs to avoid "starting a war" with the creature;

Security bars and doors will help but not stop Dogman from entering if it so wishes.[192] In fact, it has more or less lost its inhibitions to avoiding humans as a natural way of things and will not hesitate to open doors and windows or enter dwellings for whatever reason.

---

[191] Dogman Encounters with Jeffrey Nadolny, "Dogman Subscriber Call-Ins Q&A with Gov't Agent Round 2," YouTube, November 25, 2020 (3:46-4:00). Retrieved 11/28/2020: https://www.youtube.com/watch?v=MnQhPCYsmSI.

[192] Dogman Encounters with Jeffrey Nadolny, "Dogman Gov't Agent William Speaks!!! Q&A The 1st Time EP 40," YouTube, May 11, 2020 (46:20-47:20). ["William" is aka "Victor"] Retrieved 12/1/2020: https://www.youtube.com/watch?v=y3HKbDyzFbk.

Incidentally, Victor notes that trail cams are *not* effective because the Big Three *know the purposes* of the cameras (i.e. they hear and smell them) and will avoid them at all cost.

CH VIII: ONLINE MAPS CASE STUDY

One night, around January 3, 2019, some 90 days after I was first exposed to the topic of Dogman, I decided late at night, about 12:30 AM, to study an online "Google Earth" search of Taylorville, Illinois. I had read an account of an anonymous witness[193] who describes seeing a Dogman cross Lincoln Trail Road near where it crosses the Sangamon River and I had a hankering to see what I could see.

After positioning myself on the north side of the road, moving west toward the town (moving left to right on my computer screen), slowly moving along, studying the foliage for any anomalous imagery, I was stunned by what I saw: a large figure, which looked like a walking dog, following behind

---

[193] Dogman Encounters Radio, "Christian County, IL Encounter," DogmanEncounters.com, Date Unknown. Retrieved 11/26/2020: https://dogmanencounters.com/christian-county-il-encounter/.

what appeared to be a man. Both were walking west toward the town during daylight. Go ahead, laugh it up. It is what it is.

I'm not making this up. Like an idiot, I did not take a screenshot. It just did not occur to me. Back then, I didn't understand the technology I had at my fingertips.

However, I realized that I could "hunt" for these creatures online, in the safety of my home, *and take screenshots of any anomalous imagery*, and have since done that, sometimes facing ridicule and negative commentary. I was even accused of faking an image.[194]

As my friend and mentor, David S. Lifton (*NY Times* bestselling author of *Best Evidence: Disguise and Deception in the Assassination of John F. Kennedy*, 1980), astutely told me, a photograph is NOT definitive evidence. It's subjective and open

---

[194] Check out my YouTube Channel, "Boko Cafe: 'Stir Fry for the Mind'." It is an eclectic group of information. As I indicate in the description, I only post what I find interesting: JFK Assassination, Civil War History, ghosts, UFOs, cryptids, et al. Hopefully, you'll find the topics interesting, too.

to interpretation. When I see a Dogman, you see a tree stump, and the next person sees a flower petal. But, it is intriguing, and it is fun.

Do You See Anything?

(A screenshot taken November 26, 2020, 8:30 PM PT, 4100 block of Germantown Liberty Road, Germantown, Ohio, 45327)

That brings me to the point of this chapter, *Dogman Encounters Radio* (Episode 51) guest, Adam Davis of Montgomery County, near Dayton, in Southwest Ohio.[195] No stranger to the Dogman research field, he participated in a *Monster Quest* episode on the creature, Season 1, Episode 13: "American Werewolf" (January 23, 2008). Davis is also connected to the North American Dogman Project (NADP) as a co-founder and Lead Historian Field Investigator.[196]

During his DER interview, Davis mentions several specific places of geographic significance to the many Dogman sightings in that area. I believe this to be one of the most active Dogman sites

---

[195] Dogman Encounters Radio, "Dogman Encounters Episode 51," YouTube, July 15, 2015. Retrieved 11/26/2020: https://www.youtube.com/watch?v=dt0EI0oQ8Ok.
[196] NorthAmericanDogmanProject.com.

I've ever encountered in my research. It definitely rivals the voluminous Justin Turner sightings in Central Texas. Since Davis is very specific in describing location hotspots, it's easy to find these locations online as well. Odds are, you will not find anything definitive, but you never know.

As a significant sidenote, Davis' account is extremely moving particularly around 44 minutes into the interview when he describes finding shredded, bloody clothing on the side of a road. His eyewitness account (again, DER 51) is one of the most riveting ones I've ever heard - right up there with that of Brandon Close (DER 190, et al.) in upper New York State.

Thus, this episode serves as a "jump off" point if you are interested in doing online visual research of the Dogman. Searching for the Dogman, the Werewolf, Bigfoot, or what have you is certainly safer this way. I will add a little conspiratorial comment here. I think in time, Google, et al., in conjunction with the US Government, once "they" figure out that these cryptids can be discovered online viz-a-viz these search applications, will develop technology to "visually erase" or block out said cryptids in order to "protect us from this "conspiracy," or "fraud," or whatever "they" dub it. Just sayin'.

When listening to any Dogman account, if the eyewitness gives you a specific location, you can do your own visual search using whatever map application you have available.[197] I usually start at the most specific part of the location described in the interview, and then plod along the sides of the road with my mouse - analyzing the bushes and trees wherein the creatures can hide. If I see something anomalous, I enlarge the image as necessary. Plod. Analyze. Enlarge. Plod, etc. If you find something, take a screenshot.

---

[197] Top Best Alternatives, "14 Google Earth Alternatives & Similar Software," TopBestAlternatives.com, Date Unknown. Retrieved 12/29/2020: https://www.topbestalternatives.com/google-earth/.

Note that not all locations allow a close-up view. With Google Earth, for example, you can only plod along the roads which their photographing car traversed. Any views beyond that area will be limited to how much you can enlarge the image. However, you will be surprised at how much detail you can see. Here is a listing of the locations Adam Davis[198] describes and which you too can locate in a search...

---

[198] Dogman Encounters Radio, "Dogman Encounters Episode 51," YouTube, July 15, 2015. Retrieved 11/26/2020: https://www.youtube.com/watch?v=dt0EI0oQ8Ok.

LOCATION	EVIDENCE	TIME
Liberty, OH	Howling	3:47-4:50
Dayton, OH	Howling	5:08-6:02
Diamond Mill Road, Dayton, OH	Howling	10:18-10:42
Germantown Liberty Road, Germantown, OH; near the "zig zag" between Hemple Road to the north and the 4500 block of the road to the south	Dogman on side of road	16:30-17:20
Dayton Farmersville Road, Germantown, OH	Objects thrown at car, particularly the tires	36:24-38:41

Brookville, OH (north) and Germantown, OH (south) with Diamond Mill Road as a north-south axis	General observations of the existence of Dogman, i.e. footprints, smell, howls	54:15-54:27

NOTES

CH IX: INTERVIEW WITH AN EXPERT

"Mr. Hoffmann - relax - I don't care when we talk. I am not going anywhere. When it [the interview] happens, it happens."[199] This was Mr. Black's response to my nervous textual outburst just moments before.

I was very anxious to be able to speak to Mr. Black about his voluminous interactions with Dogman and Bigfoot on his property in an area which I've dubbed, "Shangri La." Since I work two jobs as well as tutoring two middle school students, it's hard to arrange time to perform such an important interview. Thus, my neurotic texts.

This man is a walking encyclopedia of Dogman and Bigfoot facts, due to the harsh reality that he lives with them on a daily

---

[199] "Mr. Black," Text to Author, Friday, January 15, 2021, circa 7:30 PM PT. This is not the real name of the interview subject.

basis. In fact, he has a detailed diary covering some two years of daily experiences with these significant creatures. Thus beginneth the lesson...

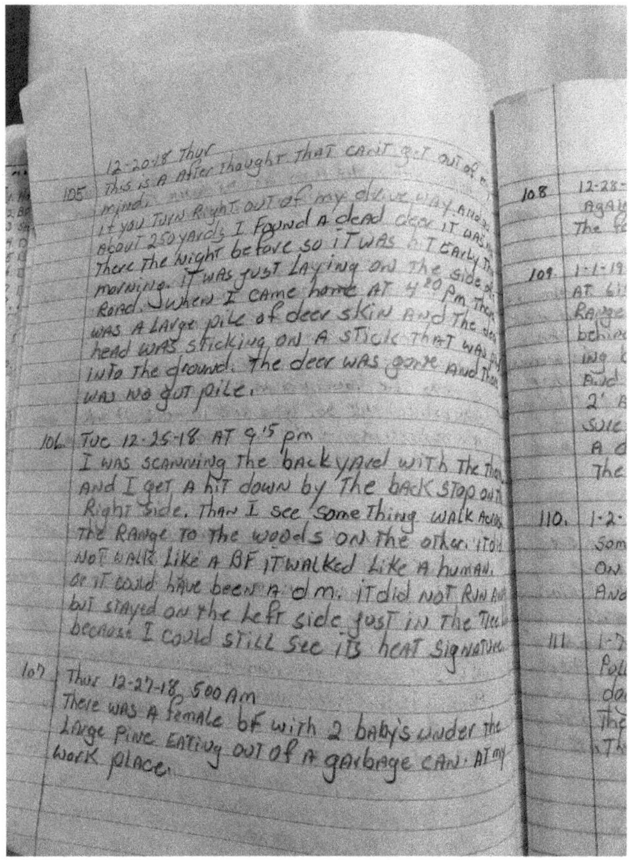

105   12-20-18 Thur

This is a after thought that can't get out of my mind. If you turn right out of my drive way. And about 250 yards I found a dead deer. it was there the night before so it was [...] early in the morning. It was just laying on the side of Road. When I came home at 4:20 pm there was a large pile of deer skin and the deer head was sticking on a stick that was [...] into the ground. The deer was gone and there was no gut pile.

106   Tue 12-25-18 at 9:15 pm

I was scanning the backyard with the th[ermal] and I get a hit down by the back stop on the right side. Than I see some thing walk across the Range to the woods on the other. it did not walk like a BF it walked like a human. or it could have been a d m. it did not run away but stayed on the left side just in the tree[line] because I could still see its heat signature.

107   Thur 12-27-18, 5:00 Am

There was a female bf with 2 baby's under the large pine eating out of a garbage can. At my work place.

(Diary Sample - Courtesy Mr. Black)

Reader, please note: Other than Victor, the U.S. Government Agent interviewed over fifty times by the podcast *Dogman Encounters with Jeffrey Nadolny*, Mr. Black is by far the most experienced Dogman and Bigfoot eyewitness I've ever encountered through my research which began unexpectedly in October 2018. Interestingly, he has lived on this property since 1995. Mr. Black currently reports 68 Dogman and Bigfoot creatures in and around this property.

My initial conversation with Mr. Black[200] was far from subtle niceties and introductions. This man is serious and he jumped right into the subject of his experiences. Though he's lived on the property for several years, over the last year (2020), it's really picked up in intensity.

Minnesota Ranchers

---

[200] "Mr. Black," Interview with Author, Friday, January 15, 2021, 7:49-9:03 PM PT.

Mr. Black has been contacted by various individuals seeking counsel on how to handle these creatures, be it Dogman or Bigfoot. One individual, a man who lives with his father and grandfather on a 1500 acre farm in Minnesota, told Mr. Black (via email) that the only way to kill the Dogman is to shoot it low (in the solar plexus, or gut), and then approach it and shoot it in the head.

But why? I learned through studying various eyewitness accounts that these creatures are extremely hard to take down with a firearm - as I noted above in the narrative. Well, according to Mr. Black's source, all three men (grandfather, father, and son) shot and killed several dogmen on their farm *and dissected them.*

What did these Minnesota ranchers find out? The Dogman has a large 1.5-2 inch thick breastplate which is practically impervious to a standard firearm round. Furthermore, the heart is actually located under the left armpit. Thus, shooting it "in the heart" like you would a human - will not work.

Filming and Photographing Dogman and Bigfoot

Mr. Black told me that he has taken literally hundreds of still photographs of both Dogman and Bigfoot but that doesn't always mean he gets a clear image of the subject creature. They can "stand in the open," Mr. Black told me, "and you can't see them." We discussed this concept a bit. Some people tend to think that because of this, the creatures must be supernatural.

U.S. Government Agent Victor, interviewed extensively by Dogman Encounters with Jeffrey Nadolny, has stated (cited above) that he knows that this notion (creatures are supernatural) is *not* true; rather these creatures achieve this ability through stealth and excellent natural camouflage. Mr. Black wholeheartedly agrees with that conclusion.

(Case in Point: Do you see the dog?)

The Vanity of Dogman and Bigfoot

Mr. Black went on to say that Bigfoot does not like to be seen, let alone be photographed, yet Dogman does not care. In fact, we discussed the issue of interaction with both, and he told me that Dogman does not care if you see him. He (or she) gets pleasure out of scaring you.

Bigfoot, on the other hand, does *not* like it when you see him to the point of threatening you when you do. Mr. Black told me that there was one time where he spotted a Bigfoot on his back porch who then became angry and retaliated by pounding on the sides of his house at night.[201]

A second Bigfoot growled and screamed loudly at Mr. Black. He says you

---

[201] Mr. Black, Interview with Author, Saturday, January 30, 2021, 11:10-12:06, PT. This is a clarification of two separate Bigfoot encounters.

feel it in the chest - the stomach and lungs vibrate. The creature tore out 1-2 inch saplings and threw them sideways like a baseball bat. Interestingly, his eyes were not glowing, "lit up." (According to Mr. Black, the Bigfoot did not appear to be angry and it appears he was just frustrated that Mr. Black spotted him.) This same Bigfoot finally chased Mr. Black onto a public road. He says it's best to pretend not to have seen a Bigfoot - if you happen to do so - for that reason. As an aside, I find it fascinating that, according to Mr. Black, the male Bigfoot keeps order, and the female Bigfoot runs the show.

Eyes "Lit Up"

One comment Mr. Black made regarded the eyes of the Dogman. He stated how the Dogman "lit up his eyes" after being approached. Frankly, I was stunned and asked for clarification. You see, I noticed that eyewitnesses don't always describe a similar set of eyes. Sure, you and I have different eye colors, but that's about the extent of the difference. Many people see the Dogman (and even the Bigfoot) with "glowing eyes" or dark black eyes. How the Hell do eyes "glow?" Why do they "glow?"

Mr. Black stated that the eyes can change colors depending on whether or not they are angry or feel threatened. In other words, if the Dogman or Bigfoot is angry or threatened, their eyes will glow.[202] In fact, he stated that this is the creature's way of warning you, of saying, "Get the Hell away from me!" *If you see their eyes in this state,* "Get out of Dodge!"

Mr. Black is so knowledgeable and detailed, he told me thusly: Dogman has several glowing eye colors such as amber, silver, blue, emerald, red. Bigfoot has a glowing red color, but also a silver color with red in the middle, and vice versa.

---

[202] Mr. Black, Interview with Author, Saturday, January 30, 2021, 11:10-12:06, PT. This is a clarification of the eye shine.

Dogman Types

Mr. Black told me that he has *personally classified* Dogman (as opposed to other more "official" classifications) into three types: Type 1 - the wolf head and body (equal to about 75% of his encounters); Type 2 - the dog head and body (equal to about 20% of his encounters); Type 3 - like a Type 2 but 2-3 times larger and built like a bodybuilder (equal to about 5% of his encounters), weighing upwards of 1500 pounds.

He added that, though the Dogman in general is extremely menacing and dangerous, the Type 2 is *most* menacing and dangerous. This grade has nothing to do with size (Type 3's are bigger), but personality. In our second interview, Mr. Black helped me to create this chart.[203]

---

[203] Mr. Black, Interview with Author, Saturday, January 23, 2021, 8:35 AM to 10:15 PT. Mr. Black insisted on clarifying his research; thus this chart.

Type 1 Dogman	Type 2 Dogman	Type 3 Dogman
Typically Wolf-like	Typically Dog-like	Typically Dog-like but larger
75% of sightings	20% of sightings	5% of sightings
150-350 lbs.	300-500 lbs. (600+ sometimes)	400-1200 lbs.
5-6.5 feet tall	6-7 (some 8) feet tall	7-12 feet tall (some 14 feet)
Head proportional to body	Head sometimes 3 times larger than body; Mane; Wolf face, Chow face, Baboon face (rare)	Head like a Type 2;

Hands black and look like a racoon	Hands grey and flesh colored with long fingers and nails (2 inches)	Hands similar to Type 1 but bigger
	Muscular like body builder	Muscles 5-10 times larger than Type 2
Travel in Packs of 4-6	Travel in packs of 2-3 (Chows always in 4)	Travel solo

Packs Versus Troops

Another statement from Mr. Black which I found rather interesting was that "packs" are homogenous groupings of Dogman, and "troops" are homogenous groupings of Bigfoot. Yet, there are heterogeneous groups of both *living in harmony*. I asked him why this could be, and he replied that it's merely a matter of survival although in such cases as a pack of Dogman and Bigfoot, the latter tends to be in charge (probably a Type 1 alpha male).

DUMB

When we breached the question of "Why do these creatures exist in such large numbers?" Mr. Black asked me sternly, "Do you know what DUMB is?" I thought he meant "dumb" as in "I'm dumb." No, that's not what he meant. This is a Deep Underground Military Base, essentially created in and around key installations throughout every state and every county.

A bit incredulous as to the government's reasoning for it, Mr. Black told me he believes these creatures are bred and released in the areas around these bases to help form a ring of protection around said bases; the citizenry's safety and security be damned.

Though I discussed this theory of government involvement in this cryptid's prevalence in our society above, and considering what Victor has already stated about said creatures above, particularly the Werewolf ("his go to warriors"), I have to agree with Mr. Black as to his reasoning, but also with Victor. Both hypotheses make complete sense to me.

Mr. Black added something which chilled me to say the least. I kind of already knew this, or believed this rather, because I have no proof. It just makes sense. He stated: "Dogman are in, Boogers are in, every county, every state, every township. They're in the inner city. You just don't know how to see them - and you have to learn how to see them."[204]

Emotional Armageddon

---

[204] Mr. Black, Interview with Author, Friday, January 15, 2021, 7:49-9:03 PM PT (17:34-17:54).

I'm blown away by Mr. Black's depth of knowledge, intellectual frankness, and soulful reality. In fact, if you truly listen to any of his accounts, he comes across as anyone's ideal grandpa, a wholeheartedly spiritual guru. Mr. Black told me a few times during our initial conversation how encountering these creatures changed his life - and not necessarily for the better. He emphatically stated: "Life's not the same anymore. I'm a different person because of it . . . You don't want to see one."[205] This statement makes me think twice about wanting to research them further in the wild. Hmm....

Additional Questions

I asked Mr. Black a couple of clarifying questions in our second interview.[206] He kindly obliged. Since I was writing down

---

[205] Ibid.
[206] Mr. Black, Interview with Author, Saturday, January 23, 2021, 8:35 AM to 10:15 PT.

what he was saying as well as interjecting questions of clarity, and Mr. Black was coincidingly agreeing or clarifying his statements and/or my interpretations thereof, what follows is not necessarily a direct quote, but the essence of Mr. Black's meaning...

JH: You stated in our first interview that, "You just don't know how to see them [Dogman and Bigfoot] - and you have to learn how to see them." Can you please explain this?

Mr. Black: You see them [Dogman and Bigfoot] a lot, but don't realize it. The photo "locks" the image in place for study. Whereas a quick-second look cannot necessarily be discerned by the naked eye, a preserved image [photo] allows the naked eye to see the creature.

JH: If you encounter a Dogman in the woods, what should you do?

Mr. Black: Don't take your eyes off of them. Don't run. Slowly back up and walk backwards. Don't yell or show teeth. Go armed. You see, in a given area, the highly aggressive ones which are prone to actually attack you, are probably rogue ones - they're new to the area. They cause the problems. The "locals" [Dogman and Bigfoot which live there] generally do not.

JH: How could someone like you deal with this on their property? What do you recommend?

Mr. Black: Don't shoot at the Bigfoot. That will start a war. With the Dogman, you need to stand your ground and not show fear. The Dogman takes delight in scaring people. You see, the Dogman is a bully. If you do not show fear, it will show its teeth, its eyes will glow (What I call the "hunting mode" - aggressive, "lit up."), even possibly pace back and forth, which is a visual sign the creature is contemplating - it does not know what to do (since you're not visibly exhibiting signs of fear).

JH: Victor suggests euthanizing them. How should we as a nation deal with this issue?

Mr. Black: Dogman is evil. They should not exist. They don't belong. It's like trying to have a pet panther in your house. That's not gonna work.

THUS ENDETH THE LESSON....

EPILOGUE

Lupus Aeternam
(Erin Johnson/Johnny Vaile Composite)

I grew up with the radio. There were still remnants of the old style radio shows on when I was little. This made an impression upon me. I see the podcast as a technical "throwback" to the days of these traditional radio shows, be they dramas or horror in nature.

This work includes citations from various sources. However, in no way am I endorsing one source over the other. If the source is not referenced herein, that does not mean it isn't good. I am amazed at the free, non-traditional, non-mainstream media sources - Alternative Media - that are available to us today.

That being said, these podcasts cost a lot of time and energy and money for the artists to create. IF POSSIBLE, please support these entrepreneurs in any way you can - be it through one-time donations, to monthly subscriptions, and/or purchasing their merchandise.

These brave artists ensure the intent and letter of the law of our blessed First

Amendment. So, if you give just five dollars per month to your favorite show, that's sixty dollars per year. These days, you will spend that amount in one trip to a fast food restaurant with your family. Which money is better spent? These sources of inspiration and excitement are free of harm and healthy for us to consume. So, in this case, I say, "Go ahead - 'supersize' me!"

Dogman Movie Poster

www.ingramcontent.com/pod-product-compliance
Lightning Source LLC
Chambersburg PA
CBHW071214240726
48654CB00009B/774